T0113927

REVELATION
son of zebedee

BY

U E WALL

ILLUSTRATIONS BY JUSTINE PETERSON

WESTBOW
PRESS®
A DIVISION OF THOMAS NELSON
& ZONDERVAN

WestBow Press books may be ordered through booksellers or by contacting:

WestBow Press
A Division of Thomas Nelson & Zondervan
1663 Liberty Drive
Bloomington, IN 47403
www.westbowpress.com
844-714-3454

ISBN: 978-1-6642-4817-5 (sc)
ISBN: 978-1-6642-4819-9 (hc)
ISBN: 978-1-6642-4818-2 (e)

Library of Congress Control Number: 2021921851

Print information available on the last page.

WestBow Press rev. date: 01/28/2022

So you will believe that Jesus is the Messiah, the Son of God, and in the act of believing, have real and eternal life in the way He personally revealed it.

—John 20:31

CONTENTS

PART I

Son of Zebedee

CHAPTER ONE

the baptizer

I remember the dream that started it: the trembling of a silver platter filled the silence, blood pooling at its rim, and a servant girl trying not to spill on the king's cobbled floor. The sickening sweet smell drifted toward her. Steady she walked. Carefully she balanced. His guards, the queen, and princess' eyes fixed on the head she carried. Trapped inside myself, I woke to the blackness of early morning. My chest rose and fell like waves in a storm. I had nightmares often, but I'd never dreamed of someone I knew. My heart pounded as I lay on my mat, remembering. I knew I would never forget seeing my teacher's bloody head on a silver platter. "In the spirit," my mother called my gift, but I didn't want it. I was twelve. The weight of knowing, of seeing the future, was too heavy.

My older brother's mat was empty, and there was no sound of my parents moving around downstairs. Late again. From the floor beside me, I snatched my tunic, pulled it over my head, and stumbled onto my tired legs.

I'll never make it back to the river before sunrise.

I pulled the door open, scraping it across the floor. Grabbing my belt from the chair, I tied it around my waist, hurried down the narrow stairway, and slipped my worn sandals on my feet.

At the end of the dirt path, I saw my brother, James. As I caught up, he raised an eyebrow at me. "Why did you come home last night, John?"

"You noticed?"

"We share the same room. What happened to the Baptizer? You aren't supposed to leave his side."

"I know that."

"So?"

"So, what?"

"So why did you sleep at home instead of the wilderness?"

"We don't sleep in the wilderness," I snapped. I couldn't tell him. He never believed my dreams.

"Well, you don't sleep indoors. He's an odd rabbi, that one."

"I'm late. I have to go." I took off running out of our fishing village to the winding path along the Jordan. I was greeted by people waiting by the river's edge. I'd never seen so many come before, though every day brought more.

I climbed down into the blue-green shallows and waded to where Rabbi rested, fiddling with my fingers. My sandal slid across the river floor. *Maybe he didn't notice I left.*

Andrew was waiting with him. He was always by his side, always did what he was told.

As the morning breeze moved across my skin, I prepared my excuse.

"Shalom, John." Andrew rested his elbow on my shoulder. "Where'd you run off to last night?"

"You're one to talk," I jabbed. "You're always leaving."

"I leave to help Simon, not just disappear. Did your father need help with his fishing?"

"No."

"So what happened?"

"Nothing." I moved and let his elbow drop.

"Nothing? You disappear in the middle of the night—for nothing?"

"Yes."

"But Rabbi didn't know you left. When I leave, I ask first."

"Well, we can't all be you, Andrew."

He smirked and said, "You mean dutifully obedient."

"Rabbi called you that *once*," I said.

"Once is enough to make it so." He elbowed me.

I closed my mouth. He was better. I didn't know why I did things wrong. I just did.

Rabbi made his way over. He towered over me, blocking the rising sun. "A *talmid* must always be close to his rabbi." He put a giant arm across my shoulder. "Otherwise, he cannot take on his character in action or thinking. Such is necessary to preserve the teachings that set us apart from the war-hungry Romans." He winked. One smile through his tangled beard always made me feel better.

I smiled back. "Yes, Rabbi." Then I saw it again. The girl trying not to look into his eyes as she carried his severed head on a platter. I jerked my head away.

He sank his hairy arms and ropelike mane beneath the surface and stood dripping in the middle of the river. He howled at the crowds from Jerusalem, Judea, and the countryside. "Look at me, a Nazarene, an outcast, but I am His. Sent by God to point out the way to the Life-Light. To show everyone where to look, who to believe in."

He drifted closer to the crowd. "All of you came to hear and see, confess sins, and be baptized into a changed life. Know that I am not here to charm with healings or to cast out demons, but to bear words of hope. You have heard the concerns about my words from our so-called leaders, but I stand before you unafraid. I am not worried what they think, only what God asks of me. Though I come from the same priesthood, I see their corruption. They are consumed by greed. Bent by money from the Romans. They have forgotten their responsibility to you." A message simple and harsh, like the desert around us.

"Change your life. God's kingdom is here."

He gestured for the first in line, and a woman with dimples stepped gently into the river. As she leaned back into Rabbi's arms, He stood firm and supported her head. "I baptize you in the name of the Father!"

I stared at her soft curls. Each strand soaked in the river while Rabbi dipped her backward into the water.

She rose, holding her hands on her chest. She staggered as she stood and strode back to the bank.

Rabbi turned around and looked at Andrew and me. "No one has ever seen God, not so much as a glimpse. My brothers and sisters, I am not the light. I am here to show you the way to the light."

"What does Rabbi mean?" I asked Andrew.

"I don't know. We're supposed to listen and watch. Rabbi says we will learn our place in time."

In time? But we've been following him for months and I don't know what I'm—

Shouting broke out on the riverside. "Make way!"

Leaders pushed through the crowd.

"Fear not, my brothers and sisters, but yes, do make way for the Pharisees, heads of our synagogues, the 'separate ones,'" Rabbi said, gesturing to them. "The learned Pharisees have come, yet again, but none more bent on my destruction than our dear Zedekiah."

Zedekiah drove his eyes through Rabbi's face. He rolled up his sleeve, exposing the prayer box tied to his crinkly arm with a leather strap. "You see this phylactery, Baptizer? It contains the hallowed scrolls that dictate our teachings. Yet what governs your words?" He pulled at it as if he imagined it wrapped around Rabbi's neck.

"This can't be good," Andrew whispered.

"They know."

"Know what, John?"

Seconds later, the Sadducees followed. Shet's bony fingers stroked his gray whiskers.

I balled my fists. Zedekiah was enough trouble, but Shet usually made things worse.

"Sons of high priests, you two? But of course." Rabbi laughed. "You honor us with your finely woven robes here in the desert." He moved closer to the water's edge. "It's rare to see both your groups united."

Shet crooked over the river, steadying himself with a walking stick, and pursed his ancient lips together. "We are united against you and your spoken traditions. We all abide in the written law that eyes can see, but it is your words that sway the masses."

"John, you know something, don't you? You always know. Why did they come?"

It wasn't the time to tell him my dream. All I could do was focus on Zedekiah.

"Can you see me, Baptizer?" He sneered. "Do you know why

we've come?" He flashed a glance at Andrew and me. "Look here, the so-called Baptizer draws young *talmidim* to his depravity."

I shrank down into the water. They were too powerful to be ignored. As I looked at Rabbi, He wasn't even blinking.

"Brood of snakes," He said. "What do you think you're doing slithering down here to the river? Do you think a little water on your snakeskins is going to make any difference? It's your life that must change, not your skin!"

"How dare you!" Zedekiah barked. "We are the children of Abraham. We are not here for your demented baptisms!"

Rabbi shook his head. "Don't think you can pull rank by claiming Abraham as father. Being a descendant of Abraham is neither here nor there. Descendants of Abraham are a dime a dozen. What counts is your life. Is it green and blossoming? Because if it's deadwood, it goes on the fire."

"Who are you? Why do you baptize in the river?" Zedekiah demanded.

Rabbi shoved his wild hair from his face. "I am not the Messiah."

Zedekiah turned his bright red face and white beard to the others. "Who does he think he is? He's insane. Look at how he speaks. He has no regard for the teachings—and forgets his place!" He whipped his head around and glared, shouting, "Who then? Elijah?"

"I am not," Rabbi answered.

"The prophet?" Shet asked.

"No."

"Who, then? We need an answer for those who sent us. Tell us something—anything!—about yourself."

Rabbi closed his eyes, taking in a deep breath. He opened them slowly, saying, "I'm thunder in the desert: 'Make the road straight for God!' I'm doing what the prophet Isaiah preached."

"If you're neither the Messiah, nor Elijah, nor the Prophet, why do you baptize?" Zedekiah asked.

"I only baptize using water. A Person you don't recognize has taken His stand in your midst. He comes after me, but He is not in second place to me. I'm not even worthy to hold His coat for Him." He turned his back to them and stretched his arms at his sides with his palms up to the sky.

I looked around, expecting the person he was talking about, but I didn't see anyone.

The leaders didn't say another word and left as quickly as they'd come.

Soon it was night, and the last person went. Andrew and I followed Rabbi a few miles from the river where he liked to camp under the stars. We unrolled our mats and lay down in the soft green grass, eating locusts and wild honey for supper. I tried not to fall asleep, afraid of my nightmares.

The next morning, I sat up, drenched in sweat, and tried to catch my breath. My hands were full of the straw from my mat. I let go, searching for my pouch of water. Desperate, I guzzled half of it, hoping to flush out the picture of Rabbi's eyes rolled to the back of his bloody head. The water filled my mouth, spilling on my face as I forced myself to swallow, looking around, unsure of where I was, but then I heard Rabbi's voice, and I knew I was safe.

Do I tell him?

When the crowd gathered at the river, Rabbi got up and hurried toward a man in the crowd. He yelled, "Here he is, God's Passover Lamb. He forgives the sins of the world! This is the man I've been talking about, 'the one who comes after me but is really ahead of me.' I knew nothing about who he was—only this: that my task has been to get Israel ready to recognize him as the God-Revealer. That is why I came here baptizing with water, giving you a good bath and scrubbing sins from your life so you can get a fresh start with God."

A good bath? Lamb of God? Here? He can't be, but Rabbi would never call someone God who wasn't. Wait. It's Jesus, from Capernaum.

Why did Rabbi say that? The scrolls say the Messiah will come from King David's family. King David's a hero, and Jesus is no king.

The teachings told of a giant, murderous and cruel, slain by the boy, David. David grew to inherit rule over all Israel. He was handsome, special. Jesus didn't look strong. His common brown tunic floated behind Him as He walked through the water. The only thing darker than it were his eyes and hair.

Andrew talked out of the corner of his mouth, saying, "It's Him! Did you hear, Rabbi? The Messiah!"

"What do we do?" Seeing the Messiah should have been a celebration, but there was no parade of horses or soldiers. And last I checked, we were still property of the Romans.

Rabbi stood there like a child seeing Caesar for the first time. It's like he could see invisible purple robes of royalty and a crown.

Jesus stood ready to be baptized.

Rabbi stepped back. "I'm the one who needs to be baptized—not You!"

Jesus said, "Do it. God's work, putting things right all these centuries, is coming together right now in this baptism."

I didn't blink, worried I might miss something.

Rabbi placed a hand behind the hair resting on Jesus's neck and the other on top of His hands held over his heart. Rabbi smiled, pressing him back into the river.

Jesus laid back weightless, closing his eyes. Rabbi lifted, and he rose from the water, smiling.

A burst of light shot across the sky. I squinted past the brightness to a break in the clouds where the stark white feathers of a dove stretched like the hem of a wedding gown. It glided down over the horizon, poised over Jesus, and then sat on his shoulder.

Jesus turned and smiled at the dove.

A voice exploded, "This is My Son, chosen and marked by My love, delight of My life."

I jumped backward, splashing about like a fish. I grabbed

Andrew's tunic, pulling myself to my feet. He was frozen in place, gawking. Everyone was fixed on Jesus. No one moved.

Before I could decide what to do, Jesus walked away, but I couldn't miss the chance. "Hurry!" I shouted at Andrew, treading water toward the riverside.

Andrew followed. We ran through the crowd—with no clue where we were going.

I looked back for a moment, wondering if we would be in trouble, but Rabbi would understand.

I saw Jesus in the distance. "He's over there … quiet," I said. I hadn't decided if I was even worthy enough to talk to Him, let alone follow Him. Surely the Messiah wouldn't want a puncher with a bad temper in His company. As I imagined Him telling me to go away, I tripped over rocks on the path.

Jesus turned toward us. "What are you after?"

"Rabbi, where are You staying?" I shuffled my feet and avoided eye contact.

"Come along and see for yourself."

CHAPTER TWO

the messiah

In His home, we sat by a fire in the courtyard. Compost burned as His mother, Mary, brought us hot meat and fresh pomegranates. He blessed God for the meal and scored the red fruit with a knife, prying out the seeds while telling us about the kingdom of God. He gave me a handful, and I shoved them into my mouth, ignoring the juice that dripped down my face. For a moment, I wasn't weighed down by my gift. I wanted to tell Him about my dreams, but I didn't know how.

He didn't ask questions about who we were or where we had been, and He smiled often.

After we ate, He explained that He wasn't ready for talmidim, and we would have to go back to Rabbi. I was hoping we could stay, but I knew Rabbi needed me. He opened the door, sending us off with a few loaves of bread and fish. I had so many questions, but they would have to wait.

Andrew and I didn't say much on the way. I think we didn't know what to say. When we got to the riverside, there was no sign of Rabbi.

"Where is he?" Andrew asked.

"He must be here somewhere. This is where he always waits." My eyes scanned the horizon. Moonlight shone on a couple in the distance, unrolling their sleeping mats near a shabby tent. We walked toward them for answers.

"Surely they've seen something," Andrew said.

The man hit two stones together over a pile of broken branches. "Excuse me?" He took his time to notice me. "What happened to the crowd?" I asked. "Where is the one they call the Baptizer?"

He didn't answer and looked back down at his task.

A gentle hand touched my shoulder. "Son," the woman said. She looked at me, tucking her hair underneath her shawl. I remembered her from the water. She was the one he baptized yesterday. "They took him," she said at last.

My dream.

"Who took him?" I said.

"The leaders. Did you not see?"

"No," Andrew interrupted. "Where is our rabbi?"

"I'm sorry, boys, but they took him away."

"Who?" I asked, raising my voice.

The man stood up, looking at me intently, and moved between us. "The leaders of the temple came with Roman guards and bound the Baptizer with rope. They took him into the city. You know what that means. He's lost to you."

My eyes welled up, and I swallowed hard.

"What do we do now, John?"

"I don't know," I whispered, replaying their words in my head.

"He is right. It's over. They'll never let him go. No Roman would free an Israelite."

I gripped the neck of his tunic, balling it in one hand. "Over? We have to get help. We have to tell our parents what Rabbi did to the King. We both know it's the only reason the Romans would ever help the leaders get rid of him. He warned us this day would come. We have to do something."

But what?

My dreams were only ever flashes of confusion—things I couldn't make sense of—but they always came true. Some I would hear about later in marketplace gossip: a fire, a drowning, a Zealot riot. Then there were some I didn't hear about: a winged beast with the head of a lion, a pale horse whose rider was named Death.

With Rabbi, no word of gossip about his death, but he was missing. Whispers floated that he was in a Roman prison. I wanted to do something, but our people didn't talk to the Romans, let alone ask them for help. The prison was a fortress, and only someone important could speak on his behalf. There was no way the governor of Judea would waste time with me. I kept silent for weeks, trying to figure out a plan, and returned to life at Abba's side.

At seven in the morning, my brother and I pulled dead fish and plants from Abba's net along the rocky shores of Galilee. The empty blue sky was my only bit of peace while I replayed how things went wrong. "What do I do, Rabbi? No one is going to believe a fisherman's son," I muttered. Saying the words was a relief. Like he could hear me.

James sat close enough to put his nose in my business. "What are you mumbling, John?"

I stared at him.

"Shalom?" He greeted me as if we hadn't been sitting next to each other all morning. "You're hiding something."

"I'm not."

He shoved past my grip on the full net, grabbing a handful of soggy muck. "I hate what we do. I don't even want to be a fisherman."

"Too bad for you. A fisherman's son can only become fisherman." I was glad he changed the subject.

"John, if we can get chosen by another rabbi, we can do what we want with our lives. It's the only way."

"Rabbis in Capernaum aren't looking for angry fifteen-year-olds like you. Besides, you don't do what Abba asks you. How can you be a talmid?"

"Any rabbi would be lucky to have me as his next in line. How hard could it be to follow the steps of an old man?"

"Harder than you think."

"But if we're chosen, we don't have to be fisherman like Abba. No more cleaning up guts left over from a night of fishing." He stood up and shook the net, uncovering more work. "We could—"

I stood up. "Rabbi is gone! They took him. He's in prison. Stop talking about it. No one gets two rabbis. We're supposed to be watching Abba so we can do this one day. That's just the way it is."

"He wasn't my rabbi. He was yours. What kind of rabbi gets himself arrested? Not the sort of thing you hear."

I glared at the tiny flecks of hair on his chin and pictured myself punching him, but Abba would be angry if we fought in front of the hired men. I rolled my shoulders back, deciding to ignore him, and walked to the edge of the water. Bending over, I cupped a handful and splashed it on my neck. "You would have stood up to them and done what was right. You never backed down," I muttered.

James walked up behind me. "You're wasting time. What are you doing?"

"Thinking."

"You do a lot of thinking, which is probably why your rabbi chose you, but you can't go back. No one can. Just don't think about it. He's as good as dead."

"Stop talking!" I moved eye to eye with him. I didn't want to talk about it ever again. I should have been there, and all I wanted to do was fix it.

"You want to hit me? Go ahead." He offered, smiling perfectly aligned teeth at me as the smell of goat cheese on his breath filled my nose. James never backed down from a fight.

"It's been weeks since tetrarch, King Antipas, ordered his arrest. He won't be able to get out. Let it go, brother."

I felt my face getting warm. "That's enough! Stop talking about it. You don't know anything!"

Then it hit me. The key to Rabbi's freedom. I knew the real reason why the Romans would help the leaders. I couldn't tell James. The truth was dangerous and would surely cause another riot. I knew what I had to do.

Hours later, we went home with Abba for supper. Most nights were spent at sea, so this was my chance to tell my parents everything. I examined our house, searching for the smooth transition into what I knew.

Stones—premium basalt plucked from the sea—now lined our house. Rabbi sat on stones in the river. The river where he witnessed them canoodling in the dark. No, that's not natural. The kitchen! Yes, the kitchen, the heart, no, center of the home … cooking with fire. Yes, fire. Their fire for one another burned until they disgraced themselves. No, that won't work—

James threw his cushion on the stone floor, knocking over my empty cup, and sat wiggling back and forth until he found the right spot. After Abba blessed God for the meal, James grabbed the ladle and heaped spoonsful of stew into his bowl without offering any to the rest of us. "Why is the Baptizer in prison, Abba?" he asked, mouth full, before I could get a word out.

My father, Zebedee, sat rooted in his seat like the trunk of a cedar tree. I could smell the sea air in his thick curls as he leaned over the table and rolled up his sleeve, exposing his sun-scorched brown skin. Everything about Abba boasted his life as a fisherman. He tore through the flatbread at the center of the table with rough fingers and tossed a piece past his round beard into dry lips. "The Baptizer was accused by King Antipas. You know things are dangerous for any man who brings change to scripture. Many have been martyred for the glory of God."

Abba answered our questions with rants about God rather than telling us plainly what he meant. It was frustrating. He wasn't one to share feelings, and he was wrong about the why.

I adjusted myself, choosing my words carefully. "Abba, that isn't the reason." I looked him in the eye. The least I could do for Rabbi was sound sure of what I knew. "There is nothing dangerous about Rabbi. I spent months with him. I know better than any—"

"I don't get it," James interrupted. "I mean, yes, he had strange beliefs … telling people 'their sins are forgiven' was unusual, different from the scribes, but why would a Roman tetrarch care? They don't even believe in our God."

Abba looked at him. "What is the position of the tetrarch?"

James sat there, taking his sweet time to answer. "To govern one of the four territories of the Roman empire—in this case, Galilee."

We weren't getting anywhere. Abba and James's back-and-forth was a waste of time. I sighed and looked at Mother's blue-green eyes. Years in the sunny courtyard had tanned her olive skin. Dark wisps of hair peeked at the edge of her veil, framing her face. I rarely saw her hair since she was careful to cover it before leaving her room each morning. I tapped her under the table.

She cleared her throat. "My sons, the Baptizer was well liked, but his behavior drew too much attention from the leaders. His arrest is a natural progression of events." She smiled and rested her hand on my bouncing knee.

"Mother ..." I said, knowing she was a safer place to voice my trouble, "I was there when Rabbi spoke against King Herod. The truth is," I swallowed a lump in my throat, "Herod was caught! He was angry for being scolded by Rabbi about Herodias and the evil things he did with her." I tried to temper my anger, but I shouted, "Herod's a coward! Rabbi told on him, in front of everyone. He knew about their affair!" I clenched my sweaty palms. "Rabbi spoke the truth when others were afraid. The people were angry. They were ready to storm the praetorium and demand the prefect remove him. If the prefect found out the people were against King Herod again, Herod would have to stab himself in the gut! But it's what he deserves!" I pounded my fist on the table. "It's disgusting. She's his sister!" I looked at my parents, worried I had gone too far.

Everyone was silent.

"When did you discover this, John?" my mother asked, her hand at her throat.

"Before the arrest. I didn't tell you Rabbi caught King Herod with his brother's wife. I couldn't. And I never thought they would come after him."

Abba pressed his lips together, leaned forward, and whispered, "Salome, sons, pay attention. I understand there was no rabbi like the Baptizer, *but* if he openly rebuked the queen, he is lost. Herodias is not to be meddled with, and she will demand his life for this. This is dangerous information. King Herod's corruption will not be tolerated by the prefect nor Caesar. He will come after you. Never again ... do you all understand?"

Abba wasn't one to discuss the personal business of others, and I saw something in his eyes I had never seen.

Abba said, "News of the affair would cause unrest and disturb an already fragile peace between our nations. Herodias will use all of her considerable influence to protect her new position as queen. Leave him in the past."

I couldn't believe it. Abba was supposed to jump from the table, rally the people, and storm the prison—not demand I keep it to myself. I didn't know what to do. *If I don't get him out of there, then my dream will come true. This is what it all meant. I should have been there. I should have done something.*

"Did you hear me?" Abba asked.

"Yes, Abba," James said.

"Of course, my love," my mother said.

"But what about Rabbi?"

"He is lost to you, to the people. Do you understand me, Johanan?"

He only called my full name when I was in trouble. "Yes … Abba." As soon as I said the words, I knew it was over.

But it can't be the end. I have to do something.

"Rabbi has been questioned by the leaders many times. No one has found fault in him. How can she hurt him? Why would anyone hurt him?" I said, hoping my words would ease my guilt. "I shouldn't have left. I could have defended him. This is all my fault," I said, wiping my cheeks with the back of my hand.

Mother put her hands on my shoulders, turning me toward her. "John, my love, this is not your fault. The Baptizer made his choice. He did so believing he served God." She hugged me.

In her arms, the flames of the stove fire in the courtyard caught my eye. There was no turning back. "Abba, may I be excused?" I asked, prying myself from her arms.

"Yes, son. Our God is in heaven doing whatever He wants to do."

I got up from the table and went down the corridor to the outside of the house. As soon as I knew they couldn't see me, I hurried up the stairs to the roof. I fell to my knees, punching the mud and clay beneath me. "He can't just rot in there. Abba's scared!" I didn't care who heard me. I paused, glaring at my torn knuckles.

Rabbi's words rang in my mind: "I'm baptizing you here in the river, turning your old life in for a kingdom life. The real action comes next: The main Character in this drama—compared to Him, I'm a mere stagehand—will ignite the kingdom life within you, a fire within you, the Holy Spirit within you, changing you from the inside out. He's going to clean house—make a clean sweep of your lives. He'll place everything true in its proper place before God; everything false He'll put out with the trash to be burned."

What does it mean? I closed my eyes, knowing the truth of my dream was coming.

CHAPTER THREE

the call

The next night, I could feel Abba's stare as I hiked myself over the rim of his wooden boat. He was a dark fog of remorse and empathy,

but no action. He wasn't going to do anything. I needed the one Rabbi prophesied.

His boat was crammed full of musky men and nets. James and I assumed our usual spots, trying to be half-heartedly useful.

"John, cast your net," Abba hollered across the open sea.

I bent down, weaved my fingers through the holes, and tossed it over the seawater like a blanket, watching as it sank beneath the frothy water. It didn't take long for us to catch something. "James, help me."

"I guess." He walked toward me with a groan.

"Don't let go this time. Abba looks to me if we drop it," I said.

"Sounds like pressure," he said. "You know, with all your strength, you still haven't figured out that no one cares about what we do."

"What do you know? You're only happy when you're doing nothing," I said, gripping the net with both hands. "Why do you come out at all?"

"Don't tell me where to be, little brother." He grunted and punched my arm.

I let go of the net, turned, and made sure to stiffen my middle knuckle as I punched him back.

He rubbed his arm. "Good one, little brother. Besides, there isn't anywhere else for a fisherman's son."

"Since you don't have a choice, why not make the best of it? Or go take a swim in the center of the sea." I laughed.

"Funny. I don't want to be here any more than you want me to be here, and it's obvious you don't want to be here either."

He was right. I wondered if Abba could tell. *Maybe that's why he keeps staring.*

Abba walked over. He looked at our net still dangling over the side of the boat, barely full, reached down and swayed his hand in the water. "Boys, use a full hand in the sea to determine the current's temperature. Where the heat meets the cooler waters, we will find God's reward."

"Why, Abba?" James asked.

I scoffed. I could see through his act. "It's where the large fish wait on the smaller."

"I knew that."

"Sure you did."

Abba sighed and walked to the other side of the boat.

"This is it," James said. "It's over for me. No matter how many rabbis are out there … they aren't going to want me. Might as well get used to what's going on here."

I didn't say anything. I figured the same thing. With an infamous, jailed rabbi and an ill temper, no one would ever choose me. We stood there for a moment and looked out at the shore.

"Work quickly, boys. The fish will not wait for idle hands," Abba shouted.

I glared down at the net, pulling it through the water. James and I lifted it up. It was barely full, just a few puny sardines and barbels. Abba only praised a net that was full of bass and perch. They had few bones and would sell for more in the market. It was James's fault. He wasn't interested in catching anything. "Can you at least pretend to work?"

"I did. Didn't you hear my question of the night? That was more than I would ever care to learn," he clarified.

All I wanted to do was hit him again. I was tired of pulling both our workloads, and James needed a good punch.

"Look over there." He pointed a few feet from us. "It's Simon and Andrew." He leaned out of the boat, gripping the edge. "Look at that hull! They can barely bring it up."

How in the world? Then again, it's Simon.

Simon was the type of person who was good at everything. He was smart, had a beautiful wife, and was the best fisherman in town. There was nothing bad anyone could say about him. He was oddly perfect, but this catch seemed too great even for him. "That's impossible," I said, watching them struggle. Something was different.

"Pull … pull harder!" Simon shouted to Andrew.

"Got it, brother!" he yelled back.

James moved closer to me as the boat sent him stumbling. "See how he listens?" He braced himself with the edge of the boat. "Andrew doesn't run his mouth like you. You always have something to say when I direct things."

I snickered. "Simon's older—and smarter. There's no way I'm going to listen to you about anything."

He shoved me. I planted both feet, ready to spring at him.

"Keep working," Abba said, catching us.

We dumped our hull on the boat floor and threw the net back in. The noise of Simon and Andrew celebrating was irritating enough without another empty net. I looked up and saw Simon jumping like a giddy girl. Suddenly he pulled his tunic over his head and leaped into the sea.

The water must have felt like rolling down a mountain nude after it snowed—and he left Andrew to row by himself. I glared into the distance as their boat moved closer to shore, following Simon's bobbing head and expert strokes to the shoreline. When he got there, he clamored to his feet and stood in front of someone. It was too dark to make out his face.

"Of all the madness. He could have drowned. What's so important?" James asked, breathing in my ear.

I could see torches dancing on the horizon, and I heard cheering directed toward a single person at the edge of crowd. They halted their celebration to look across the water at our boat.

I froze.

James crooked his head. "Are they looking at us? It feels like they're looking at us."

"No," I said. "Why would they be?"

When Andrew reached the shore, the man they celebrated boarded Simon's boat. He, Simon, and Andrew rowed back out just a few feet from the shoreline.

The crowd closed in around them and looked out to their boat.

He started gesturing and speaking, but it was faint whispers from where we were.

All stood listening from the edge of the water, and James and I were really distracted. Every few seconds, he looked over at us.

"Are you sure they aren't looking at us?" James asked. "That's Simon and Andrew." His eyes bulged from his head, trying to make out the faces in the dimness. "And someone else. If only he would turn around and stand in the light."

I was interested, but I knew it wouldn't be long before Abba saw us. I had disappointed him enough. He could always pierce the night with a single glare and make me feel like a scolded babe without a word.

"Focus, James," I said, swatting him on the arm with the back of my hand. "We need to pull up our net and see if we got anything. Our fortune fishing is not about to change by ogling Simon's boat. If we don't catch something soon, Abba will make us stay out here all night."

"Yes, Simon, the mighty fisherman," James said.

"Here we go again."

"Go again with what?"

"You're jealous."

"Jealous? Why would I be?" He crossed his arms. "We're the same height, *almost*."

"You're much, much skinnier," I said.

He sent a firm upward fist to my stomach, and the swift intensity felt like the air had been forced from my throat all at once. "It's not my fault Abba compares me to him in everything. He's older—not bigger!"

"He's only three years older," I said in a choked voice.

"Yes, eighteen going on forty."

I exhaled. "So he speaks ahead of most of us. He's still a nice person."

"The only thing more striking than his dark hair and skin is his big mouth."

"Days on the hot shore, he's earned his trademark." I stiffened my stomach enough to stand up.

"I didn't hit you that hard," he said, looking me over.

We went right back to studying the other side of the sea. Simon was soaking wet in his boat, rubbing his arms. Soon all three returned to shore and built a fire in front of the crowd.

"Why are they just standing there not working? They must have given up. There's no fish out here tonight," James said.

"A sea with no fish?" I looked around. Abba and the other men grappled another empty net, soaking the boat's surface.

James seized a torchlight fixed to the edge of the boat, trying to get a better look at the man speaking.

I squinted into the distance, surprised that Andrew wasn't working either. He had picked up some of Rabbi's free-spirited practices and stopped combing his hair, an homage of sorts. We didn't talk much anymore. All he wanted to do was relive the good old days with Rabbi, and I wanted to do something about his arrest. I didn't want to diminish our friendship; it just sort of happened.

"Where have we seen the other one?" James asked.

I knew James wasn't going to let it go, so I looked over the water to the other man. As James held the fire outward, I could make out the tunic and tassels hanging from his outer garment and shoulder-length hair. I felt odd looking in his direction, but something was familiar about the way he commanded the attention of every person on the shore.

"We know him from somewhere. We have definitely seen him before, but it's hard to tell ... it's so black," James said, about to fall overboard.

I gripped his arm. "It's a small town. We know everyone."

Then something unexpected happened. We heard it. The man called out to us. I wasn't sure at first, but then I heard it again.

How does he know my name? Rabbi? It can't be ... can it?

I stood there, ready. My soul cried out across miles of seawater. *Rabbi?* I refused to look at Abba, worried my loyalty to him would make me stay. I had to answer the call from across the water. What if was the Baptizer? What if he needed me? I could see the crowd on the shore. Surely they raided the prison, demanding his innocence, and that's why they were celebrating. He came back for me, called for me, but why James? Didn't matter. This was it. The kind of moment that turned mistakes into providence. For once, my dreams were wrong. I was so eager I didn't stop to ask James what he thought. After all, his life was his own, and he needed to choose for himself. I filled my lungs with all the breath I would need to make it back to the surface and immediately, without a word, I jumped overboard, leaving Abba in the boat with the hired men.

The harsh cold surrounded me as I plummeted into the deep, guided upward by a sliver of moonlight. Exhaling, I emerged, striking the surface for samples of air. I couldn't see who called me or what was waiting, but I was drawn to it. My heart ached with every stride forward, wondering if Rabbi would be angry. There was little time to catch my breath, but I kept going faster and faster.

Finally, my hands clawed the shore's surface, and I lay there shivering and breathless. The world spun as I fixed my stare on my bluish hands and rose to my knees. I rubbed my arms and dropped them to my sides, too tired to warm myself. Moments later, I heard gasping behind me.

"John, John. He called me too," James huffed, half alive.

We walked forward, united for an unknown cause, suddenly surrounded by a crowd. I felt the awkwardness of many eyes examining my person.

But who called?

"This is where all the fish went!" James shouted, tripping over the bounty.

Thousands were entangled in the net. I made my way through the crowd to Andrew's familiar face. "What happened? Where did you find all this?" I asked, observing the torn seams. "How did you not sink? Are you hurt?" James was right; it was as if all the fish in the sea were in that net.

The crowd made way, leaving room for the one who called. *Jesus!* In an instant, I was very pleased—but I was also confused. I didn't know why He called me. It had been so long since I'd seen Him. Forty days at least—I counted. He looked the same, but there was a strange light in his eye. I didn't know what to say.

"Come with Me. I'll make a new kind of fisherman out of you. I'll show you how to catch men and women instead of perch and bass," He said.

With so few words, we were freed from a life at sea. I turned and looked back, searching for Abba's boat. There he was, in the distance, holding his torch out toward us. My attention split in that moment. I would miss the life I knew, but I couldn't go back. Following the Messiah meant an unknown future, a petrifying thought, but for the first time in a long time, I was hopeful.

Jesus took one look up and said, "You're John's son, Simon? From now on, your name is Cephas."

James raised an eyebrow. "Rock?" he muttered.

It was a moment of honor. Jesus was now our Rabbi, and in His role, He renamed His talmid. By changing Simon's name to Peter, Jesus revealed that he would be of great importance to His ministry.

Before I could decide if I should leave, Jesus gestured for us to follow. With that, the four of us left our lives behind.

CHAPTER FOUR

following him

We walked through the vast greenery covering northern Galilee. My tracks over His, careful to be like Him in every way. It was an extraordinary thing looking at His face, the Messiah. I always thought He would be taller, rich even, but I had no doubt that His kind words and smile belonged to a king. He spoke of His kingdom as we walked through a rainbow of wildflowers. Kneeling, He cradled a carmelite flower between two fingers, describing the glory of heaven with the same way someone my age would. His voice was full of excitement about what His Father would soon reveal.

As I saw the rolling peaks, so different from the rocky streets I knew, I wondered if His home looked like ours. Inhaling the scent of the meadow, I took it all in. I knew this moment was important, chosen by the King. My hands got sweaty when He said my name or asked me a question. I couldn't help but wonder, *Why me?* I shook my head, marveling at the opportunity to call Him Rabbi.

Wind carried the sea air and cedar as we went down a strange trail. A landing of trees stretched forever, with woven branches holding each other upright, casting huge shadows. At the center, a boy sat and ate alone. He looked like the sort who couldn't run without getting winded a minute into it. I watched him, while Rabbi and Peter stopped ahead.

Andrew came up behind me.

I asked, "What's he doing here?"

"I know him!" Andrew blurted. "It's Philip, from home."

James butted in and said, "You have another brother?"

"No, I mean Bethsaida. He is from where we are."

"Why is he out here alone?" I asked.

"He's always by himself." Andrew hurried over to Peter and Rabbi. "That's Philip, right?"

Peter squinted into the distance. "It looks like it. You know he keeps to himself."

Rabbi went toward him, and we followed. We stood around the tree, but he didn't look up, only stuffed what he was eating under his satchel. Rabbi knelt beside him. "Come, follow Me."

Philip stared with his mouth open. A piece of chewed bread fell out.

Say something.

"Is he deaf?" James whispered.

I shrugged.

Philip swallowed hard. "Yes, Rabbi," he said finally.

Andrew reached out a hand, helping him to his feet.

Philip clutched his full sack to his chest, and Rabbi continued through the trees.

"Shalom. I'm John, and this is my brother James. Philip, right?" I said, hoping to break the silence.

"Yes," he answered, looking at his feet. "You're Andrew, Simon's brother?"

"Yes, but it's Peter now." Andrew winked.

"What do you mean?"

"Rabbi said so," he explained.

"I see." Philip nodded.

"Peter means rock, you know?" Andrew added, chest puffed.

"So Rabbi wants him to be in charge?" Philip asked. "Is that why he and Rabbi walk ahead of the group?"

"Technically, he's second. Rabbi's in charge," James interjected. "I could have been second."

"Second?" I laughed.

James checked to see if Rabbi was watching and then punched me in the arm.

"What?" I said, rubbing the spot.

"Peter's the oldest and the only one who's married. Renaming him means he's special," Andrew added. "It means *he* is second. Anyone who doesn't like it can ask Rabbi."

No one said anything. Questioning Rabbi was not acceptable.

"How old are you?" I asked, changing the subject.

"Thirteen, almost fourteen."

James cackled. "Still the youngest."

"Does it matter?" I was irritated that someone so small and round could be older, even though I had no reason to be.

"What were you doing out here alone?" asked James.

"Nothing. I like to come out here to think."

"More like to eat," James said, looking him over.

Philip looked at the ground again as if it were going to help him. He wiped the evidence from his face. "I forgot to eat before I left home."

"Doesn't look like you're the type to miss a meal," James said, patting him swiftly on the back.

Philip stumbled forward, dropping his sack.

I crouched down to help him pick up a pomegranate as it rolled away. "Don't listen to him."

He grabbed figs, bread, and fish, tucking them back inside, and smiled awkwardly. "A light snack for later." He laughed timidly. "So you've all heard the stories?"

Andrew made a face at him. "Stories?"

"About Rabbi and what He's done?" Philip answered as he stood up.

I dusted dirt from my palm and stood. "Stories about what? We all know what is written about the Messiah."

We continued on. Philip turned to the three of us as if he were about to reveal the mysteries of creation and said, "No, not what the scrolls say. What He's done all over town."

"Like what?" James asked.

"He speaks to *demons* … calls them by name … or rather they know Him. A friend told me He can touch you—"

"Calls them by name? Ridiculous," James said.

Andrew stopped walking. "What do you mean by calls them?"

"Gossip. You sound like a bunch of girls. The marketplace is full of nonsense stories. No reason to get worked up," I explained. Part of me wanted to know more, but the idea that stories were spreading only ever meant trouble.

"It's not gossip," Philip said. "People have seen things. Rabbi's different. The things He can do are unlike anyone else. The demons know Him."

Know Him?

Before long, we made it to another clearing—a farm of fig trees on the outskirts of town. I stayed a few feet behind everyone, thinking about what Philip had said.

"Let's get some!" James said as he reached for his sack. He hurried to Rabbi and asked if we could pick a few, which was proper, and Rabbi nodded.

Hunger pangs were a welcome distraction from the thought of demonic possession, as if my dreams weren't enough, but I needed to know more. Our eyes met as I watched Philip add more food to his sack.

"So how did you find the Messiah?" he asked me.

"I followed Rabbi before, but He wasn't ready for talmidim, so Andrew and I went home. We didn't know it was Him until we swam ashore. There were so many fish."

"Wait. What happened? Why did you swim?" he asked.

I reached up next to me, plucking a single fig and held it to my mouth, thinking. I knew my story was jumbled, but I couldn't focus. The thought of demons felt weirdly familiar. Was that why I dreamed of a dark future? Was that why my mind was full of troubled promises rather than adventure?

"Shalom?" he said, snapping his fingers at my nose.

I said, "Rabbi got into Simon's—I mean Peter's boat. We couldn't see what happened. They looked like they were going to sink. Rabbi called to us, and we jumped out. When we reached the shore, there were fish everywhere! We'd never seen anything like it. Never. Good fish too. Huge ones. Enough to feed all of Capernaum. It was incredible."

"This is so crazy. No one will believe this back home. Philip, me ... with the Messiah."

"I feel the same way," I said, looking at Rabbi.

Philip pointed in the distance. "Look, over there. It's Nathanael!"

"Nathanael?" I asked.

He ran off toward a boy sitting under a tree at the edge of the clearing. I went with him, curious about the coincidence.

When I arrived, Philip was bent over, hands on his knees, about to collapse. "Nathanael!"

Nathanael sat up a bit, stretching out on his mat. He held back shoulder-length hair with a hand, glaring with eyes as green as the leaves surrounding his face. "Philip?" he said. "What are you doing out here? And you've made a friend?"

Philip stood up, huffing. "We've found the One Moses wrote of in the Law, the One preached by the prophets. It's Jesus, Joseph's son, the one from Nazareth!"

I thought Rabbi was from Capernaum.

"Wait." Nathanael rose to his feet, nearly the height of the whole tree. "Nazareth? You've got to be kidding."

Nazareth was a tiny town in Galilee—and nothing happened there. The prophecies said nothing of the Messiah coming from there. None of it made sense. The Baptizer didn't lie.

"Nazarenes are bushmen and outlaws. You remember the Baptizer? What a joke." Nathanael said, rolling his eyes.

"Shut your mouth! The Baptizer was no joke!" I shouted, balling my fists. "He wasn't an outlaw. They lied against him." I slid my right foot behind me.

"He's imprisoned for a reason. The Nazarenes are wild men with big stories. You two should be more careful what you believe in," he continued. "What you're claiming doesn't make sense. Do you even listen in the temple? The Messiah is to be born in Bethlehem."

I moved closer. "We know that!" I was ready to punch him in the face.

"Well, if you know that, why would you think you found Him?" he said, unbothered by my advance.

"John, it's fine," Philip said, moving between us. "Come, see for yourself." He grabbed Nathanael's arm, leading him away. Nathanael kept an eye on me as I followed them to the others.

As we approached, Rabbi looked at him. "There's a real Israelite, not a false bone in his body."

Nathanael stopped short. "Where did You get that idea? You don't know me."

"One day, long before Philip called you here, I saw you under the fig tree."

"But you couldn't have seen me ..." Nathanael exclaimed, "Rabbi! You are the Son of God, the King of Israel!."

"You've become a believer simply because I say I saw you one day sitting under the fig tree? You haven't seen anything yet! Before this is over, you're going to see heaven open and God's angels descending to the Son of Man and ascending again."

We all looked up. No one moved. Then Rabbi turned and walked away, and we followed.

Soon the sun began to set, and we gave our attention to unpacking our sleeping mats under the trees. We feasted on figs and bread. Peter reached out his hand, welcoming Nathanael to the group.

That night, I gazed at the stars and thought, *Angels and demons?*

In my dream, I saw a man dressed in clean shining linen with a golden sash around his chest. He was surrounded by more like him, armed in a place made of light. "Michael ... Michael ... Michael," they chanted behind him.

At the edge of the light were the ones they would battle: men with torn faces, singed robes, and a nub at the top of each shoulder, where something was missing. They were commanded by a huge and fiery dragon with seven heads, ten horns, and a crown on each of the seven heads.

War broke out. Michael and his angels fought the dragon. The dragon and his angels fought back, but they were no match for Michael.

The images were so clear. I didn't know why it was important, but I sensed it was. When I woke, I wanted to tell Rabbi, but I worried my dreams meant I was possessed. *Surely, He wouldn't want me if I am.*

Sunrise brought the Sabbath, and our group continued to the bottom of the mountainside. I yawned and slapped my cheeks. Lifting my sandals, I hoped the cold grass on my toes would keep me awake. I didn't know what to do. I looked ahead at the others, envious. They seemed to have the one thing I didn't: peace.

Andrew lagged behind them, dragging his feet. We weren't used to long hours on the road. Being a fisherman meant staying close to sea, and we only ever left for the yearly celebrations in Jerusalem.

I picked my pace up to talk to him. "Rabbi isn't like the others, is He? What they said He can do will change everything."

He smiled and nodded. "You look terrible, John."

"Thank you."

"No offense, but you look like you didn't sleep."

"I didn't."

"Another dream?" He put his hand on my shoulder as we walked. "What did you see?"

James looked back at us and stopped to let us catch up to him. "What are you two talking about?"

"John had another dream," he said, dropping his hand to his side.

"Not again. I told you, brother, coincidences aren't providence."

"They're more than coincidences. Name one that hasn't happened," Andrew said sternly.

"It doesn't matter. What you're suggesting doesn't happen anymore. People don't prophesy."

"What was the dream, John?" Andrew asked.

I didn't tell them about my regular dream of the Baptizer's head. Saying the words out loud felt like asking for it to come true. That was the one I wanted to figure out. I knew the new one from last night would settle his questions.

"So?" James demanded.

I sighed. "I dreamed of war."

We stopped walking. James tossed his hands up. "War? With the Romans? How prophetic. Oh, wait. They're always at war, murdering for the glory of land. Well, we belong to them. I would say they've won."

"Not the Romans."

"Don't listen to him. A war where, John?" Andrew had the same face my mother had when I told her about my dreams, something between curiosity and confusion.

"I dreamed of a war. Thousands fighting."

"Again, *so?*" James asked, scrunching his face.

"A war fought by the angels and a dragon."

"A dragon!" James laughed.

"The dragon was the ancient serpent, the one called devil and Satan!" I shouted, defending and surprising myself. *Wait? How did I know who the dragon was?*

Neither said a word. I looked ahead, hoping the others didn't hear my outburst. No one else did. "There was a beast with horns, and seven heads, and a crown with bear paws and a lion's mouth." As the words left me in chaos, I felt like I could float. Like the words were not my own and saying them freed me of their burden—if only just for a moment.

James blinked repeatedly. "You dreamed of Satan? A beast with seven heads?"

Andrew gave me a look. "I'm sorry, John."

"I don't need pity or questions. It's the same as always. Dreams that don't make sense." The burdened returned like a boulder falling from the sky. I looked at their faces. Their reaction was the exact reason I kept my dreams myself.

Andrew put his hand on my shoulder again. "Tell Rabbi, John."

James pushed him aside and stood in front of me. "No! He'll get rid of you. Don't you dare. He'll think you're possessed."

Andrew shook his head. "He rids people of possession."

"Where did you hear that? The fat kid? No, he's confused. Don't listen to them, John."

"How does the way Philip looks change the value of what he said? Grow up. This is what we've wanted for a long time: a rabbi who lets us be ourselves. Why shouldn't I tell Him?"

"And if you're wrong? And He sends you away?"

The thought of His rejection made my stomach hurt. James was right. My dreams and thoughts were too strange for anyone to accept. Even my own mother avoided my detailed stories. I was sure the Messiah would be disgusted at my thoughts. I couldn't tell Him. It was my burden to carry.

"He's not the Baptizer. No matter how much you wish He was," James added. His words felt like a dagger in my gut. I clenched my teeth and balled my hands.

James looked at my fists. "Look, all I'm saying is that we left behind everything we know. Can't you forget your dreams like everybody does?"

I didn't realize we had stopped following Rabbi. My words were an unwanted deterrence to being an obedient talmid.

Philip came over and said, "What's going on?"

"No one was talking to you," James answered with a glare.

Andrew shook his head at James. "James has questions about Rabbi's ability to call out demons."

"Don't worry. You don't have to be afraid," Philip said.

"I'm not afraid. None of us knows what He can do," James asserted.

"Speak for yourself," Andrew said. "Word has spread about Rabbi's miracles and how He heals the sick by simply touching them. No one agrees with you. What do you believe, if not the Messiah, and why follow in disbelief?"

James looked over at Andrew. "I believe in the Messiah," he said, moving in front of him. "The scrolls say He will overcome the pagans and rebuild the temple, but the temple doesn't need rebuilding. None of this makes sense."

I released my fists and grabbed James's arm, jerking him away from Andrew. I knew what he was going to do.

"Let go," James said, glaring at me.

I let go and stepped back. I realized James had shifted from being tactless to voicing his concerns about following Rabbi. I wanted to side with him, but he was wrong. I looked ahead at Peter and Rabbi still making their way down the mountain. We were far behind, and I was a relieved Rabbi didn't hear any of it.

"Don't do it, brother," James said. "Your dreams of death and destruction have only ever brought you trouble. Whether He can help you or not remains to be seen."

"James, people are often afraid of anything or anyone different, but we don't have to be," Philip interjected.

"Enough!" I shouted.

Rabbi and Peter stopped walking, waiting for us to catch up.

Immediately, they ran to Him, and I made my way behind them. We reached the edge of the road. I stood there behind the others, ashamed.

He gestured for me to come forward.

"Yes, Rabbi," I said, moving toward Him.

He put His arm around my shoulder. The anger of the argument dissipated as we stood at the top of a hill. In the seconds of silence, I felt as though I had shared all the previous moment's frustrations with Him. I inhaled the familiar aroma of the sea. "Rabbi, why are we home?" I asked.

He stood with Capernaum on the horizon as the sun rose. He smiled and outstretched His hand toward town. "I have to tell the Message of God's kingdom, that this is the work God sent me to do."

CHAPTER FIVE

demons

We reached the foot of the hill. Home, the city of comfort, nestled along a heavily trafficked Roman highway. Soldiers trampled past, carrying spoils of taxes and goods seized in the name of Caesar. I couldn't help but wonder if the only reason we traveled through the mountain pass was to find Philip and Nathanael.

Was He collecting talmidim? And what for?

The sun triumphed high with no clouds to protect us from its warmth, yet the early start of autumn provided a breeze as we moved through the city gates behind Rabbi. He led us to the most important dwelling at the center of our village: the synagogue.

Roars from the shofar called our people to hear traditional readings from the scrolls. As we scaled the hallowed basalt stone stairway, I took in the familiar beauty of etched pillars adorning the entrance. In the corner near the doorway, a group stared at Rabbi, pointing in His direction. His reputation created a lure, and they stalked us inside. Their interest reminded me of the Baptizer. I hadn't forgotten about my first rabbi—or given up on his release. I just figured I would ask for help when the time was right. I didn't want to tip the boat, so to speak.

Dimness surrounded the seven-branched candle menorah on the altar, and the important men took their seats on stone benches surrounding the prayer hall. We stepped through the crowd seated on the floor and made our way to the front of the room.

There he was, Zedekiah, seated among the other Pharisees. I hadn't seen him in a while. His lavish robe, woven from a single stream of cloth, revolted me like incense on a pig. I hated him. He was the reason for so many sleepless nights. Then the Sadducees followed, slithering in with floor-length tunics and golden chest plates.

Our people struggled to feed their families and survive the bloodthirsty Romans, but these frauds thrived here at our expense.

Rabbi turned around at looked at me. *Can He sense my anger?*

The synagogue was no place for resentment; it was a place of contrition and learning. I refocused, staring through the crowd, hopeful that I might see my parents, but there were too many people to pick out faces in the dim room. I gave up, leaning against a pillar next to Andrew and James, as the opening blessings were recited.

Our old schoolteacher, Naaman, known as hazzan, entered. He stood steady for an old man of bone and skin. His clothes were as ill fitted as his temper, and he brooked no nonsense in the temple, gazing around the room, ensuring complete silence. He took his position on the bema. Uncurling his crooked back, he shouted the Shema, "Attention, Israel! God, our God! God the one and only! Love God, your God, with your whole heart: love Him with all that's in you, love Him with all you've got!" He carefully unrolled the delicate animal skin scroll, preparing the Haphtarah according to schedule.

Zedekiah rose—it was his role to read the selection from the prophets—and he whipped his head back and glowered at Rabbi. "Deeply respect God, your God. Serve and worship Him exclusively. Back up your promises with His name only. Don't fool around with other gods, the gods of your neighbors, because God, your God, who is alive among you is a jealous God. Don't provoke Him."

Rabbi walked to the bema and stood in front of him.

Zedekiah stiffened with both eyebrows raised, and I held my breath. The last person who had interrupted Zedekiah was in prison.

Rabbi rolled up the scroll. "Let me tell you why you are here," He said, looking at the people. "You're here to be salt-seasoning that brings out the God-flavors of this earth. If you lose your saltiness, how will people taste godliness? You've lost your usefulness and will end up in the garbage."

I waited. Calling the leaders corrupt was beyond bold—it was defiant. Everyone watched, starved for Rabbi's explanation.

"Here's another way to put it: You're here to be light, bringing out the God-colors in the world. God is not a secret to be kept." He shook His head, addressing the crowd. "We're going public with this, as public as a city on a hill. If I make you light-bearers, you don't think I'm going to hide you under a bucket, do you? I'm putting you on a light stand. Now that I've put you there on a hilltop, on a light stand—shine! Keep open house; be generous with your lives.

By opening up to others, you'll prompt people to open up with God, this generous Father in heaven."

Nathanael stepped closer to us and leaned into my ear. "I can't believe His radical and unapologetic words."

James said looked around the room and said, "They pierce every ear."

Andrew said, "Yet His words are as a father to his children, warning of harmful behavior and—"

"Demanding personal change," Philip said, finishing his words.

Rabbi patted the scroll and said, "Don't suppose for a minute that I have come to demolish the scriptures—either God's Law or the prophets. I'm not here to demolish but to complete. I am going to put it all together, pull it all together in a vast panorama. God's Law is more real and lasting than the stars in the sky and the ground at your feet. Long after stars burn out and earth wears out, God's Law will be alive and working.

"Trivialize even the smallest item in God's Law, and you will only have trivialized yourself, but take it seriously, show the way for others, and you will find honor in the kingdom. Unless you do far better than the Pharisees in the matters of right living, you won't know the first thing about entering the kingdom."

Heads turned to the leaders, waiting for a rebuttal. James and I looked at each other and then to the leader's red faces.

Surely they'll defend themselves.

Not a word. Rabbi shifted His gaze between the leaders and people and said, "And when you come before God, don't turn that into a theatrical production either. All these people making a regular show out of their prayers, hoping for stardom! Do you think God sits in a box seat?

"Here's what I want you to do: Find a quiet, secluded place so you won't be tempted to role-play before God. Just be there as simply and honestly as you can manage. The focus will shift from you to God, and you will begin to sense His grace.

"The world is full of so-called prayer warriors who are prayer ignorant. They're full of formulas and programs and advice, peddling techniques for getting what you want from God. Don't fall for that nonsense."

Shet shifted, scowling in his seat, and then stood. "Who do you—"

The room went dark. The menorah lit itself, the flames dancing as if they were being blown out. "James," I whispered, a heavy feeling in my stomach, "did you see that?"

"See wh—?"

Wind swept through the room, tossing hair and clothing. The crowd stirred. Then again. In the shadows at the back of the room, something crept along the floor between two pillars. Soft breaths, moist and hot, moved between us.

"Quit it, Andrew!" James demanded.

"Quit what?"

"Don't touch me!"

"I didn't touch you," he said, looking at him.

The pungent smell of sulfur filled the room, like eggs left to rot in the sun, but worse. It felt like it burnt the hairs in my nose. My eyes watered as the room succumbed to forceful coughs and gagging, but no one moved for the door.

The slumped figure drifted closer ... closer, contorting itself upright.

Rolling it shoulders backward, it came to the light. Exposed, the white pupil-less eyes and the darkened face of a man squirmed. Gripping a bloodstained shawl, he revealed sliced wrists. His head bobbled with scabs where hair should have been. His withered frame creaked as he dragged his mangled foot, inch by inch, closer— careful to avoid more light—until he stood face-to-face with Rabbi.

Several voices started yelling.

"What business do You have here with us, Jesus? Nazarene! I know what You're up to! You're the Holy One of God, and You've come to destroy us!"

All eyes locked onto the gruesome stranger.

I tried to look past tears as the light flickered over his cracked skin and torn cheeks. His fingernails were caked with blood. "Look at his hands," I whispered, disoriented.

"Blood?" James asked in a shaky voice.

"He's been tearing his own skin," I replied.

"Why?" Nathanael whispered.

Andrew gripped his throat. "What's wrong with him?"

"Did he say *us*?" I asked.

Rabbi stood firm while the man smirked with black teeth. His head thwarted side to side, unhinged. "What business do You have here with us, Jesus?" Giggling manically, his body suspended in midair like a puppet on strings. Foam and saliva seeped from clenched teeth, and he stared right into me. The legion of impure spirits trapped within, contorted his arms and legs, bending them unnaturally backward. I covered my ears at the sound of snapping bone. Joints protruded through his skin.

The sight sent everyone pushing and shoving frantically to the door. We stood united with Rabbi. He stretched His hand toward the man and commanded, "Quiet! Get out of him!"

He fell, slamming onto the stone floor, and demonic spirits shot out from his body like black clouds. Fleeing, they wedged between the stones, burrowing into the ground. Seconds of silence. His chest rose forcefully, expanding. He gasped and color returned to his pale skin. Scratches faded, and his bones reset to normal.

The few remaining in the synagogue looked at Rabbi with wide eyes.

An old man hiding underneath the leader's bench stood and shouted, "What's going on here?"

A woman cowering in the corner grappled shakily to her knees. "A new teaching that does what it says?"

Another man pointed, "He shuts up defiling, demonic spirits and sends them packing!"

Rabbi gestured for us to draw near, and He led us out of the temple without discussion.

I didn't know what to say. I couldn't believe what had happened, and it was clear by the silence that no one else did either.

As we headed through town, images of his broken body and the shrill screams rushed around my mind. I didn't know how Rabbi did it. I stared at Him as He moved calmly down a paved road. *How did the demons know His name?*

CHAPTER SIX

miracles

It was the not knowing that bothered me. My eyes searched the streets, sure the possessed lurked between the houses. Replaying the exorcism, I looked at Rabbi and wondered how to keep my questions to myself. I didn't even realize we had come to a familiar place until we came to the door. Being there should have brought comfort, but I felt like there something wrong inside.

Andrew came up behind me. "Why are we at my house?"

A demon.

Nathanael looked at him. "Is anyone in your family ... like that man?"

"I don't think so. Wouldn't I know?" Andrew answered.

I shrugged, glaring at the wooden door.

James stood at my side. "Why are we here?" he whispered.

We waited while Rabbi and Peter spoke outside the door, hesitating. Every passing moment felt like it was building up to something awful, but I needed to know why we were there. Then it struck me like a slap on the back of the neck: *He's the Messiah.* We left the temple safely, and it seemed dumb to forget. I looked at my friends' troubled faces. "We're tired, and it'll be nice to get off the road," I said to them.

They looked at me and then at each other.

"A good meal is exactly what we need," I said, trying to persuade them. I knew there was no way they would pass. "On the other side of this door is flatbread, cheese, fresh pomegranates—"

Peter opened the door. "Come on in."

I prepared myself, every sense needed to be ready. I saw the large timber chest where we used to laugh and joke with Peter and Andrew's family, eating like there was no tomorrow. The room felt quieter than before, while the oil lamp shone half-heartedly over a few of their father's carvings—its flickering brought me back to the unease of the temple. My heavy scanning of the front room was interrupted by the warmness of caraway and ginger flowing in the air.

James shoved me. "Look." He pointed to a figure in the corner.

At the far side of the house, something was in a messy bed.

Not again.

Rabbi went right toward it, and we followed. For seconds,

I could only make out black crinkled hair, with slivers of gray, collected into a braid against white ... *clothing*—and then a face shielded by the darkened corner. A woman. I glared harder, looking for sores or signs of struggle, but instead found forgiving wrinkles that reminded me of Mother. Pale skin drenched in sweat, didn't appear possessed, but sick.

Drawing her blanket toward her neck, she stiffened and smiled. "Shalom. Please forgive my appearance. My energy escapes me. I was not aware you were coming," she said, looking at Peter.

"Yes, Simon didn't tell us You were coming, Rabbi," Peter's wife said from the courtyard. "Shalom, you're most welcome," she said to us.

My mind wandered across her slim nose and green eyes. I swallowed, trying to look away, but I couldn't help staring at her pink lips as she smiled at me. "Shalom, John, Andrew." My stomach flipped as she embraced me. "And who do we have here?"

"Nathanael," he said, ogling her.

"And you?" she asked, smiling.

Philip glared at the floor. "I—I'm Philip."

"I'm glad you've all come. Mother isn't herself," she said to Rabbi. "We've tried everything. Nothing's helped."

"Yes, Rabbi. I received word a day ago. She's been sick for some time," Peter added.

Rabbi walked to the bedside with a smile bright enough to light the room. He bent over her, carefully reaching out His arm. Taking her hand, He helped her up.

She stood along the bed, stretching her arms. Color filled her skin. "I feel like myself again." She looked at her feet. Sliding on her sandals, she smiled at Rabbi. "Thank you," she said, lingering in His presence.

It was as if they were speaking to each other without another word. Walking over to the bowls, she began gathering them. I was excited as she collected a clay pot from the chest and went outside to an open fire at the back of the house.

Not long after, we were all laughing and eating, surrounding the table in a rare, uninterrupted moment with Rabbi. It felt like home, a family, and it was Rabbi who had brought us together. I smiled at Him, deciding it was time to ask my questions. "Rabbi, what happened in the synagogue? How did the demon know Your name?"

He looked up from His pomegranate seeds and piled a few more into His mouth, looking around the table. He gestured a hand across Peter's mother's spread of finest reserves of wine, fruit, and handmade deliciousness. "If you decide for God, living a life of God worship, it follows that you don't fuss about what's on the table at mealtimes or whether the clothes in your closet are in fashion. There is far more to your life than the food you put in your stomach, more to your outer appearance than the clothes you hang on your body."

It wasn't what I wanted to hear. I needed an explanation—about how everything happened or would happen. Distracting myself from all the questions I wanted to blurt out, I stared outside, thinking about what He had said.

A small sparrow landed in the courtyard. It was free, troubled with only its search for scraps along the dirt.

He called my name. "Look at the birds, free and unfettered, not tied down to a job description, careless in the care of God. And you count far more to Him than birds. Has anyone by fussing in front of the mirror ever gotten taller by so much as an inch?" Reclining, silent for a moment, He looked at us. "What I'm trying to do here is to get you to relax, to not be so preoccupied with getting, so you can respond to God's giving. People who don't know God and the way He works fuss over these things, but you know both God and how He works. Steep your life in God reality, God initiative, and God provisions. Don't worry about missing out. You'll find all your everyday human concerns will be met. Give your entire attention to what God is doing right now, and don't get worked up about what may or may not happen tomorrow. God will help you deal with whatever hard things come up when the time comes."

He was right. It seemed like only yesterday that the Baptizer was arrested. The Baptizer. I realized I no longer called him Rabbi. So much had happened since then. I'd let go and never really thought about why it felt like it was the time do so, but it was—because of Rabbi. If He could call out the demons by name and send them running, then I could rely on Him for where to go next. It was much easier than worrying. I leaned back on the floor and popped a date into my mouth.

The others seemed satisfied with His words.

Peter raised his cup and said, "I'm thankful for this meal and the rest. Thank you, Rabbi."

Rabbi bowed His head to His chest. I couldn't help but feel fascinated by His humility. He didn't boast about the miracle of healing the demon-possessed man or Peter's mother; He wanted the focus to remain on God. The Messiah didn't come to be praised or storm the fortress of the Romans; He came to teach. It wasn't what I expected.

Evening came, and Peter's mother closed the back doors leading to the courtyard as a cool breeze moved through the room.

"Want to go out front, John?" Andrew asked.

"Sure." We got up and went to the front of the house while Peter's wife and Rabbi cleared the table.

Brightness from the setting sun shone as we opened the door. I squinted, stepping outside.

"John, why are all these people here?" Andrew asked.

Hundreds waited.

"Where is your Rabbi?" a woman asked.

A little boy broke free from the crowd. "We heard He knows the demons. Is it so?" he asked, tugging on my tunic.

An old woman crooked over her cane. "Son, can He really heal me?"

It seemed the whole town surrounded us. Rabbi came to the door, walking past Andrew and me. Many stepped forward, bringing sick relatives and friends, and others brought those who were inhabited by demons. The other talmidim joined us at the door. Soon, Rabbi began to cure each one. I moved to the edge of the crowd, watching as He called the spirits out by name from their victims, but He wouldn't let the demons speak.

After every miracle, the crowd rejoiced. When anyone left, ten or more came in their place.

By the time they had all gone, it was late. Rabbi instructed Peter to prepare a place for us to sleep. We went inside and laid out our travel sacks. As I spread my mat, I couldn't help but wonder why Rabbi wouldn't let the demons speak.

I awoke at daybreak. Yawning loudly, I stretched my legs across my mat, thinking about the people Rabbi had healed. The room was a huddle of blankets and tossed about tunics, but I didn't see Him.

Where did He go? The latrine? It's early.

I waited a moment, then another, but He didn't come.

"James—*James*," I panicked. "Where's Rabbi?" I said, tossing off my blanket.

"What? Why are you being so loud?" he mumbled.

"Rabbi. He's gone."

"No, He's not. What did He tell you yesterday about your worrying, John?"

"But I waited. Something's wrong. What do we do?"

"I don't know. Be quiet. Not everything is a crisis, John. He's here somewhere." He turned over.

"Leave it to you to be more worried about sleeping." I said. "We're only traveling with someone who draws more of a crowd than the Baptizer, but you're right; why worry? He disappeared into the air. No chance the leaders took Him."

He sighed. "Let's find Him." Sitting up, he rustled through his sack and grabbed his tunic. He pulled it over his head, hopping while trying to put on his sandals. "Where could He be?"

Peter sat up with one eye closed. "What are you two doing—other than making noise? You'll wake Rabbi. He had a long day, or didn't you notice? He needs—"

"Peter, He's gone," I interrupted. "They took Him while we slept!"

"There were plenty of faces in the crowd I didn't trust," James interjected.

I grabbed my cloak from the floor and threw it across my shoulders. "We're going to look for Him," I said.

Peter stood up and got dressed. "John, get the others," he instructed. "Andrew, we need to leave. Get up!"

Andrew propped himself up on his mat. "I'm up," he answered, grabbing his things.

I hurried out to the other room where Philip and Nathanael slept. "Get up," I demanded.

Once they were dressed, we went to others.

Peter looked at us said, "We don't have time for questions. We need to leave and find Rabbi. Move quickly."

His home was still dark. Peter stopped for a moment and took his wife's hand, smiling at her. She didn't ask when we would be back or insist that he stay. She smiled, standing in the doorway until we disappeared down the street.

Nathanael said, "It's unlawful to take a person at night. The people won't stand for this."

"Pick up the pace," Peter said.

Philip looked at him. "It's not likely He was arrested at night."

"Whoever took Him did it in secret. We need to keep our eyes open," Peter answered. "We'll look for a crowd, even though it's still early, it's our best chance."

We moved quickly down the empty streets. Before long, we reached the city gates and made our way out to the wilderness, circling back and forth through common paths. I couldn't shake the similarities between my rabbis. *It isn't fair. I barely had any time with Him. I should have been awake. How could I sleep through His arrest? I'm so dumb. I should have known better. I let the Messiah get kidnapped. What are my dark dreams worth if they couldn't see this coming? Just give me one more chance, God, and I'll never leave His side. I'll protect Him. Don't let this be it. I need to do something.*

"We've been circling for an hour," I said, catching up to James. "Does Peter even know where he's going?"

"I don't know, but there's no use fighting. We have to be calm," James answered.

"When did you start relying on Peter? Are you trying to impress him? Of all the times to accept him as leader, why now?"

James said, "Impress Peter? Why would I care about that? He should have been watching to see when Rabbi left."

"This is a waste of time. Rabbi is in danger, and we're taking a walk!" I shouted, looking ahead at Peter. "We should be going to the prison!"

"The prison?" Philip asked with a scrunched face. "No one can be arrested without a trial."

"No one?" I asked, raising an eyebrow. "That's exactly what they did with the Baptizer. Are you ignorant?"

Peter stopped walking. "John, you're only making things worse."

"No, he's not," James said. "He's right. This is a complete waste of time. This isn't the way to find Rabbi."

Andrew moved in front of James. "Who are *you*? It isn't your choice. You're not going to tell us how to find Him."

"I'm not? Of course, you wouldn't naysay your brother—even when he's clearly wrong." James glared down at Andrew's forehead.

"Can't you shut your mouth, for once?" Andrew said through clenched teeth.

"I can help you shut yours," James warned.

"Enough! James, now is not the time for one of your fights." Peter moved in front of Andrew. "I don't have time to argue. You can all go back to bed. I'll look myself."

Peter's face was bright red, and I'd never seen him so upset. His normal confident posture had shifted to a sunken chest. "You're right, Peter, but we should stick together," I said, regretting the trouble I had caused. "Rabbi called us together, and we should stay—"

"Finally!" Peter interrupted, pointing ahead.

In the distance, by the light of the rising sun, there He was.

Peter ran to Him, like a lost child to his father.

Rabbi patted Peter on the back, and they came toward us. "Let's go to the rest of the villages so I can preach there also. This is why I've come."

As soon as He said it, it became clear. Rabbi hadn't come to sleep in or to perform miracles; He was there to preach the truth. Rabbi explained that He had gone to a secluded place to pray. The discipline and self-control it took to go to God so early was something I didn't do, but I knew it was why He was different than everybody else.

James walked up beside me. "Don't ever wake me up again." He shoved me.

I realized it was harder to let go than I thought. Every moment was unexpected. I couldn't shake the worry. It was stuck to me. Rabbi's teachings were dangerous, and now we were supposed to spread it everywhere. I didn't know if I could face the leaders again.

CHAPTER SEVEN

healing

Winter brought snow to the hills of Galilee. We spent the passing months in nearby villages sharing the truth of the kingdom to come, healing the sick and maimed, and driving out demons. As time rolled on, my fear of the possessed seemed to retreat to the back of my mind, but my dreams were worse. The more we fought the darkness, the closer it felt.

One morning, Peter, Nathanael, and I went to the marketplace for food while Rabbi taught the people in the center of town. I felt the darkness like a shadow behind me, and all I wanted to do was get back to Rabbi. The others were content looking through the options, smiling at carts of fresh fish, warm bread, and fruit cooled by the desert air.

I noticed Peter's glazed eyes as he held a loaf of bread in his hands. "Hungry?" I said with a smirk. "We haven't even paid yet."

"Eating makes me happy," he said, grabbing a few more pieces of bread and fish. He weighed the food on a balance, deciding what the group needed.

Nathanael shuffled through the money bag. He hesitated as we approached the merchant. "John," he whispered, "we don't have enough."

I gave Nathanael a firm pat on the back. "It'll be fine. See if we have a few rion. That's all we need."

Nathanael rolled his eyes. "We're always short on money. We're going to starve."

"Nathanael, we're doing something more important than filling our bellies. We can't survive on bread alone," I reminded.

He handed the merchant a single rion; it was enough to buy the bread. "You're right," he conceded.

I wrapped it in a cloth and put it in my hide sack. Looking through the market, I searched for a crowd. "Rabbi's over there. Come on."

As we made our way over, the crowd began to hurry away from Rabbi. I couldn't see what was coming.

A woman grabbed her daughter and shouted, "Unclean! Hurry, let's get out of here!"

Then I heard it again. "Unclean!" someone else cried, pointing down the road.

There, at the end of the street, a man limped toward Rabbi. "Look," I said to the others.

Nathanael grabbed my arm. "No, John. We need to get out of here. It's forbidden. We can't go to Him."

"I'm not going to stay here. Stay if you want," I answered.

Peter shrugged at Nathanael. "He's right. If Rabbi is unafraid, so should we."

Before long, the center of town was cleared, leaving Rabbi and us. Others kept their distance and hid in their homes. A few lingered in the alleyways, covering their mouths with their shawls.

Then he, a leper—host to a vile disease—stood before us. His mashed face, covered in craters and pus, seemed miserable. I'd never seen one this close—nor ever for that matter. Every inch of him surprised me. His swollen brow oozed into his mouth, which was fused shut by tumorous blisters. I winced at the lumps that disfigured his face and hands. I felt rude staring, but the sight of his bloodstained tunic made it hard.

When I managed to take notice of the rest of the group, James was covering his nose and mouth with his sleeve. The stench of rotting flesh grew stronger as he moved closer. I was afraid to move.

James slid behind me. "What is he doing ... out here? He'll be stoned."

"He must know that ... but it doesn't look like he cares," I said, trying to hold my breath. We held our ground, staying close to Rabbi.

The leper lifted his tunic to his face. Falling to his knees, he wailed, "If you want to, You can cleanse me."

Rabbi put out His hand, touched him, and said, "I want to be clean."

The lumps and sores vanished, and he stopped crying.

Rabbi said, "Don't talk about this all over town. Just quietly present your healed self to the priest, along with the offering ordered by Moses. Your cleansed and obedient life, not your words, will bear witness to what I have done."

He got up and ran down the empty street with not so much as a thank you, but clear streets meant rest. Rabbi led us to a quiet place outside of town. We nestled ourselves under a cedar tree. I reached in, brought out the bread, and handed it to Him.

"Are we going to talk about what happened?" James whispered to me.

"Why? We know there's nothing He can't do. Today's no different," I replied.

Not long after, I stretched out, leaning against the trunk, considering the leper. *Strange to leave the leper caves just for a chance to be healed. I guess he had no choice. A sad life—no family, no people to love—but now he's free because of Rabbi. A new man. Will he keep it secret? Secret. My secret. My dreams. The darkness is so close. Maybe Rabbi can cure me. Rid me of dreaming of death and war.*

Someone moved in the distance, then another, and Rabbi pointed to the crowd making its way toward us. He knew they were coming, but He seemed unbothered.

The others saw them and hurried, packing their spread of dates and bread.

"Here we go," James said.

A woman approached us and shouted, "There He is!"

"Hurry, everyone. He is the One who healed the leper," an old man added.

"A leper? How?" another asked with wide eyes.

"By simply touching him. The leper told me. He is fully healed!" the man answered.

A man in fine robes ran to us with open arms. "Quickly, let us go and see who He is."

As more came, they pressed our group toward the tree. We stood, about to be trampled. I felt my heart racing.

"The leper told," James said, trying to grab his things from the ground.

Philip pouted. "There goes our rest."

"Look at desperation. People from all walks," Andrew said, examining them.

James said, "This swarm won't budge until they've had their moment with Rabbi. It'll take all night."

"We're here for them," Andrew said.

"He wasn't supposed to tell. Now, look," James said, glaring.

Rabbi began touching the heads of those who were sick, healing them instantly. He cradled babies with fevers and touched the spine of an old man. He encouraged and healed until the sun set.

In the moonlight, I tried to stay awake, sure the leaders were among the crowd. There were many new faces, and not all were happy. A few of the elders stood on the outskirts, staring at Him. They paced back and forth around the crowd, whispering to one another.

"Spies," I said, swatting Peter.

He stood on the balls of his feet, looking above the people. "Come with me."

We hid behind a tree a few feet away.

They stood with icy stares. "Who does He think He is?" one said.

"When the crowd disperses, we will report to Zedekiah and the others. We must preserve the teachings," a second replied with arms crossed.

"It's the same as the Baptizer. This is how it all started," I whispered to Peter.

"Rabbi is not the Baptizer, John. Even though I do not trust their decisive talk, that's all it ever is: talk."

He was making excuses, but I knew better. I only hoped one of the others would agree with me. I left Peter's pointless watching and headed back to the group. "We need to protect Rabbi," I said to Philip, James, and Nathanael, standing behind Rabbi. Andrew was at His side.

"Protect? What are you talking about?" Nathanael asked.

"Look," John said, pointing. "Peter's over there right now while the leaders' spies plot their report to Zedekiah and Shet. They won't stand for this many people listening to Rabbi."

"He's right. We knew Rabbi's message would make the leaders angry. It's only a matter of time," James added.

Andrew came over. "Why is Peter over there?"

"He's watching the scheming leadership," James answered, scowling at them.

Peter returned.

"So?" I asked.

He waited a moment. "Listen, we need to try not to worry."

"But you're worried, aren't you, brother?" Andrew asked.

"Uneasy," he said, looking back at the leaders. "Change is never welcome. We need to be very careful."

Philip put a hand on Peter's shoulder. "You've seen what Rabbi can do—have faith. Everything will be fine."

"Everyone knows what Rabbi can do, and that's the problem. Things will never be the same," James said.

Peter looked at the people and then the leaders. "Things were never meant to be the same."

News spread of the leper, forcing our group into the desert. We could no longer move freely through town. Those loyal to Rabbi met us to hear Him teach in the mountain passes. People flocked from all over, searching for us, including the leaders. The other talmidim and I did our best to focus on Rabbi, committing His teachings to memory, but we were on edge, wanting to be ready for anything.

One afternoon in Capernaum, after weeks in hiding, we made our way to Peter's house.

"I'm ready to relax," James said. "I didn't think we'd ever be in a home again."

I shook my head. "We were safe out there. Here, the leaders can watch our every move."

"Yes, but Rabbi has already said when we get there, our stay will be brief. So all we need to do is be quick," James answered.

Philip pointed to the house. "Oh, no. Look, at the—"

"Of course!" James interrupted, tossing his hands up. "What are they doing here? How did they know we were coming, Peter? You told your wife, and she's told the entire town!"

"No, I didn't. They must have spread word from the city gates."

Rabbi came up behind our silent grumbling, put a hand on Peter's shoulder, and gestured forward.

Hundreds parted way, allowing us through. Peter sighed, opening the door to Rabbi, and we went inside. "I'm not about to let this crowd stop me from rest and a meal," James said, pushing me forward. "Quickly, John."

The crowd didn't wait for an invitation into the house and followed us inside.

"How do they always know?" Andrew asked as more poured in from the street.

They filled the home to the point of bursting, and people were standing or sitting in every part of the home. Even the doorway was sealed with people. I could barely move. Struggling to step over men, women, and children, I sat close to Rabbi on a mat in the family room.

Rabbi stood up and began teaching.

Bits of dirt and straw fell into my hair from above. I looked up to the sound of dried branches crinkling as larger pieces fell around us.

Ambush!

I couldn't do anything. There wasn't enough room to stand, let alone jump into attack. Clamoring to my knees, I tugged at Peter's tunic. "What's happening?"

Peter glared at the destruction with a red face. Someone was on the roof, digging furiously between the planks. The entire house became silent, focused on the larger clumps of earth falling, but Rabbi did and said nothing, only staring up.

Light peered through the opening, but it was soon covered by a flat object, lowering down.

A mat?

Four men sat on the roof. I looked around the house. There was no other way inside. It was an act of desperation. Lower and lower, until the mat rested inches above His head.

Rabbi stepped aside, making room, and those on the roof settled it on the ground. And there he was, covered in straw and mud, looking up at Rabbi.

What's this? He must want something. Why is he just lying there?

Rabbi looked at him. "Cheer up, son. I forgive your sins." He bent down to the man.

"Wait!" a familiar voice shouted from the crowd. The hazzan. He pushed past a few people, nearly falling on his bony legs. "Why does He talk like that?" he shouted, shaking a finger through the air. "Why, that's blasphemy!"

Rabbi's statement was punishable by death. I swallowed as more leaders emerged from the crowd with curled lips. They muttered among themselves.

"Why this gossipy whispering? Which do you think is simpler to say: 'I forgive your sins' or 'Get up and walk'? Well, just so it's clear that I'm the Son of Man and authorized to do either—or both." Rabbi smiled at the man on the mat, offered both hands, and lifted the man. "Get up. Take your bed and go home."

As Rabbi rose, so did the man. He stood in amazement of his own legs, smiling ear to ear. He waved to his friends on the roof, and they disappeared from the hole.

In full view of everyone, the man knelt down, took his mat, and walked through the crowd.

I inspected his legs.

The people started talking as they created way for him.

"It's amazing!" a young girl in the crowd said, clutching her chest. "Who is this Man?"

"The Son of Man?" another asked.

An elderly man stood up and said, "God has given Him authority to perform this healing among us!"

The leaders huddled in a circle, whispering to one another again. I tried to focus on the dividing groups as the man worked his way to the front of the house. Some tried to touch him, wondering if their eyes deceived them.

Then the hazzan stepped forward and bared his teeth. "Those who remain in this home, uniting mind and eyes with this heretical teaching, will be reported to the chief priest. We will note all who stay!"

All eyes were on him.

"Did you hear me? I am taking note! I know your faces, families, and children by name. Go, now!"

With that, the people began to disperse. By nightfall, there was no one left. An unwelcome patron to the temple was as good as a leper. The chief priest had the power to destroy one's reputation and business with a single glance, but we stayed with Rabbi.

Later that night, Peter's wife prepared a small meal. There was little talk at the table. Rabbi seemed to be reflecting, talking even, but He said no words. It was as if He could hear the voice of Someone else.

After supper, Peter and Rabbi stayed behind and instructed the rest of us to get some sleep. We went to the back of the house and got ready.

I opened my mat, spreading it on the ground, and the others undressed and were soon fast asleep. "James," I whispered.

"What?"

"Rabbi's in trouble. The leaders are planning something. They were so angry. What do we do?"

"What can be done? Rabbi understands the weight of His words, and this isn't the first time," James said.

"So we wait for them to accuse Him? Let Him be taken like they took the Baptizer? I won't let that happen. You know that, James. There is no reason for their plotting and nonsense!"

James turned to me and said, "I agree, but that hardly changes the way things are. Relax, little brother. We will keep an eye out. If things get worse, we can always leave."

"Leave?" I scoffed. "Are you crazy? We can't leave. He's the Messiah. Where would we go? Back to fish?"

"I'm not sure like you, John. I don't know if I'm ready to risk my life. I care about Rabbi, but the thought of dying alone in a dark prison is more than I can handle. We can make it on our own."

"I've made it clear to you: I'm *not* leaving Him. What part of that don't you understand? I mean it, James, no matter what." I turned away, biting my lip. There was no reason to leave. The thought of traveling without James made me feel sick. I didn't want to say anything else.

James said, "Take the blasphemer outside the camp. All those who heard him are to lay their hands on his head, and the entire assembly is to stone him. Say to the Israelites: 'Anyone who curses their God will be held responsible; anyone who blasphemes the name of the Lord is to be put to death. The entire assembly must stone them. Whether foreigner or native-born, when they blaspheme the Name, they are to be put to death."

The words rattled me. I knew the law.

"John … John?" He sighed. "Fine, but we know putting oneself on the same level as God will not be overlooked by the leaders—or the people."

"I know the teachings!" I shouted, flipping over.

Peter opened the door. "What are you doing? Go to sleep! We have a long trip ahead." He turned and left.

"Rabbi knows the teachings," I whispered. "You're not listening," I said, trying to sound clear. "Fine. I'll handle things on my own."

CHAPTER EIGHT

sermon on the mount

Weeks later, we traveled along a route by the sea, followed by thousands. My sandals filled with water as we began our hike up a mountaintop. They were still damp when Rabbi stopped, sitting on a large rock etched by the water's path. I leaned against it, and He began teaching on subjects of moral importance. I listened as best I could, pausing every few moments to investigate the crowd. My fidgeting must have been a dead giveaway that something was wrong because Andrew was staring at me. "What's with you?" he asked.

"I didn't get much sleep," I lied. The truth was my dreams had become the least of my worries. After all, despite constantly seeing the Baptizer's blood-soaked head, it hadn't happened. Maybe James was right. Maybe my dreams were just a few lucky guesses.

"John?" he pressed.

"What?" I answered, bouncing my knee.

"What's the matter? Dreams?"

I glanced at him. "Everyone dreams, Andrew. I'm not even sure how you can sleep."

"What do you mean?"

"Rabbi's in danger."

"He doesn't need our protection. Things won't end the same as they did for the Baptizer. You don't need to worry."

He didn't know. He was a coward. They all were. The entire crowd was full of drifters and outcasts. Any of them could be scouts, and all the others did was dismiss it.

Rabbi stood. "Don't pick on people, jump on their failures, criticize their faults—unless, of course, you want the same treatment."

Uh-oh.

"That critical Spirit has a way of boomeranging. It's easy to see a smudge on your neighbor's face and be oblivious to the ugly sneer on your own."

I slumped. Somehow, He always knew what I was thinking, good or bad.

He stood up and walked between the people. "Do you have the nerve to say, 'Let me wash your face for you,' when your own face is distorted by contempt? It's this whole traveling road-show mentality all over again, playing a holier-than-thou part instead of just living your part. Wipe that ugly sneer off your own face, and you might be fit to offer a washcloth to your neighbor."

Rabbi was right. Andrew had every reason to feel safe with Him, the Messiah, and I was spending so much energy worrying about what hadn't happened. I turned to Andrew. "You're right."

He grinned.

I forced a smile back. Although I wasn't convinced Rabbi was safe, I regretted judging him. I propped myself up on the rock. Pressing into the rough edges of it, I tried to ease the stress of more people climbing the mountain to see Rabbi. I knew there wasn't anything I could do if someone turned against Him, and it made me feel horrible.

"I'm speaking to you as dear friends. Don't be bluffed into silence or insincerity by the threats of religious bullies. True, they can kill you, but then what can they do? There's nothing they can do to your soul, your core being. Save your fear for God, who holds your entire life—body and soul—in His hands.

"What's the price of two or three pet canaries? Some loose change, right? But God never overlooks a single one. And he pays even greater attention to you, down to the last detail—even numbering the hairs on your head! So don't be intimidated by all this bully talk. You're worth more than a million canaries."

There it was. The reason I had nothing to fear.

When Rabbi finished, He led us down the mountain and into town to eat. The people followed. We were always going to be surrounded.

Let go. I need to let go.

"Thief!" a gruff voice shouted.

I hurried to Rabbi's side.

I know that voice.

"You're nothing but a dirty, rotten, stinking thief!" A huge man, with dark skin and a red face pounded a heavy fist on a tax collector's table. "You're skimming profits!" he said, leaning over.

"Annas, be calm," his wife pleaded, grabbing his arm.

"No! I've had enough of his lies. He's a traitor!"

We followed Rabbi as He circled the tax collector's booths at the center of the marketplace. I tried to see the face of the man who was yelling through the crowd.

Abba's friend, Annas.

He was one of the wealthiest men in town, and he was known for his rage. He had served as high priest the year before and given the position to his son-in-law, Caiaphas. Abba and he had been friends for years. I'd seen him angry before, but the vein beating in his neck meant whoever pushed him was in for it.

"Look at me, Levi! Look at me well." He pointed to his eye. "I paid you, yet we receive word we aren't current. My family stands before you. *Make* this right!"

The tax collector sat up in his seat, barely big enough to defend himself. He wasn't much older than me. His round hat centered in brown hair, feeding into black scruff. He cleared his throat. "Annas, you *are* wealthy—and Rome demands its due."

"What did you say?"

Levi tapped his fingers on the edge of the table. "You know the penalty if you refuse. What would you have me do, pay for you? I'm a child. What's a mere shekel to a man of your status? Several days' wages? For any other, giving it would be impossible, but for you, it's nothing."

Annas grabbed Levi's tunic, balling it in one hand. "I'm not letting you get away with this!"

"Annas, no," his wife whispered, pulling his other arm. "The Romans," she warned.

"Rome cannot save you from the wrath of God!" He jerked Levi forward. "Do what is right!"

Levi tried to pry his shawl free. "I can't help you, Annas. My hands are tied."

Centurion soldiers pushed past, making their way over. "Here they come, my love," Annas's wife warned again. "Please, it's not worth your life. They'll kill you. Please, pay him and let's go."

He let go and looked around at the people watching. Reaching into his sack, he tossed several denarii into the air.

The coins flew, hitting the table and ground. Levi lunged forward, clamoring to catch them. Then he bent down, crawling across the dirt, and gathered every coin.

"Filthy beggar!" Annas said, glaring at him. He and his wife turned around to leave, pushing past Rabbi and us.

I waited for Rabbi's reaction. He stood there, quietly observing Levi. I couldn't help but feel sickened as he searched like a dog looking for a bone.

"Why do tax collectors reject our laws and cheat their own people?" James whispered to Peter.

Peter shrugged.

Rabbi walked closer, and we followed. We might as well have been walking into fire. Everyone was staring at us.

Rabbi placed both hands on Levi's table as he took his seat.

Levi stared wide-eyed, mouth opened, and then he looked down and stared at the table.

Rabbi placed a hand on Levi's chin, lifting it upward. "Come along with Me."

Levi cocked his head. "*Me?*"

A woman in line to pay held a spread palm on her chest.

As I looked around, there were horrified and wilted expressions. Our group was silent.

Levi stood up, and we made our way through the marketplace with a tax collector.

We hadn't gone far when Levi asked, "Rabbi, will you come to my house? I would like to repay Your kindness. No one usually speaks to me. I mean, usually they're upset if and when they do." He laughed nervously. "I don't have much, but I have food. Plenty for all of you."

I held my breath.

Rabbi agreed and turned to the rest of us, eyeing our repulsed expressions. We exchanged them for awkward smiles and followed Levi home.

Why risk his company? The leaders will be furious.

James came up behind me as we came to the door. "Now we dine with sinners," he whispered.

"Rabbi has His reasons." I glared down the road, hoping we weren't being followed.

Levi opened the door to a lonely existence. Inside a few pots and kettles, a single seat and a cobwebbed fireplace waited.

"I expected more from a life spent cheating," James muttered.

The door creaked closed behind us, disrupting the emptiness. There were no children, no family, no warm greetings.

Even the lepers have each other.

Levi lit a melted candle above the stove and began collecting things for the meal.

The rest of us, except Rabbi, huddled around each other like the home was a leper's cave. "Where's his family?" Philip asked out of the corner of his mouth.

"This place might as well be plagued with locusts. If anyone finds us here, we are done for," James said, looking around.

"This is the life of a thief?" Andrew whispered.

"Sad. A life of stolen wealth isn't worth this," Nathanael replied. "He's a prisoner."

I didn't know what to say.

Rabbi, on the other hand, was smiling. He walked around like something was hidden behind the dank walls.

Levi said, "Please, let's eat in the courtyard. I haven't eaten there in some time, and it's not too cold." He gestured outside to a small wooden table.

James touched the single chair. "No wonder he steals," he muttered.

"I have two mats, three cushions, and a hide. One for each of you." He smiled and pointed.

Nathanael pursed his lips. "That's oddly precise."

Levi began preparing supper, and we gathered the seating.

I heard whispers behind me, coming from a square window at the back of the courtyard. *They followed us.*

We sat down, watching the faces peek through the window.

A woman wrinkled her forehead and shouted, "Come and see." She signaled to someone behind her. "See who He dines with? A tax collector."

"Levi has stolen from me for years, and they eat as if he's family," another added.

Zedekiah poked his giant nose through and eavesdropped. All the miracles and positive stories about Rabbi left him little room for criticism—but eating with a tax collector was the thing he needed.

Rabbi walked to the stove, carrying an empty bowl, and Levi smiled as he filled it. "Seven pomegranates, forty olives, three pieces of bread, and enough cheese for each of us," he said.

Rabbi nodded, brought it to the table, and handed it to Peter.

"John? *John,* take it," Peter said.

I didn't move. I waited for Zedekiah to do what he did. He looked at Peter, a few feet from the window, and said, "You are His student, are you not?"

Peter turned to him.

"What kind of example is this, acting cozy with the riffraff?"

I waited for Peter's defense, but he just lowered his head.

Rabbi came and stood behind Peter, turning to Zedekiah and those in the street. "Who needs a doctor: the healthy or the sick? I'm here inviting the sin sick, not the spiritually fit."

Even though Rabbi had explained many times how He wasn't there for the people boasting of their own goodness, they still didn't get it. He came to serve those in need of something bigger than themselves, those willing to accept they lacked too much to be whole alone.

My opinion of Levi went against everything Rabbi said or did. The healing of the sick, the lepers, the demon possessed—all of it showed that He valued every person.

Rabbi sat down, blessed God, tore a piece of bread, and passed it to Peter.

Zedekiah said nothing and left, and the crowd went with him.

The sun set over the courtyard as we ate, letting go of previous troubles. Before long, we were laughing and telling stories.

Levi looked around the table. "Rabbi, thank You for coming. Thank You for being kind," he said. "Unlike many, my family didn't have a trade I could learn, so I suppose becoming a tax collector seemed like an easy fix. I thought it would save me from life on the streets, but it wasn't long before everyone saw me as nothing. I lost everything, but now, Rabbi, I see that I can be more. This is the first time in a long time that I've laughed."

Rabbi placed His hand over Levi's.

"Please, stay tonight. There's plenty of room."

Rabbi nodded. He and Levi stood up and began clearing the table, and the rest of us went inside.

In the main house, we found a place to rest. I took my usual spot next to James and unrolled my mat. "Can you believe this, John? Brothers with a tax collector," he said, sitting down.

"If Rabbi would choose you, then a tax collector is no problem," I teased.

"Funny, but I'm not the one the high priest hates."

"He's not high priest anymore."

"Remember what Abba said, 'He'll always be in control of the people.'"

I knelt down. Taking off my tunic, I rolled it into a ball, placed it at the top of my mat, and sat down.

Levi came in with the others. "Thank you for agreeing to stay. I know it's not what any of you had in mind, but I'm grateful."

Peter patted him on the back. "Thank you, Levi. It's nice to have a home to rest in."

"It's Matthew. Rabbi changed it," he added.

"Gift of the Lord. It's a good fit," I said. I hoped the name would give him something to live up to.

On my mat, I folded my arms behind my head and rested them on my tunic.

"*Gift?* More like a burden," James whispered to me. "Not sure how he's our equal. What has he done to deserve that? I don't trust him."

I sighed, closing my eyes. "Rabbi taught us to accept each other."

"I may be wrong about what he deserves, but the leaders will use this against Rabbi. They already had enough reason to stone all of us."

I laid there.

"John?"

I turned away. He was right.

"Did you hear me? Things will only get harder with a tax collector."

There in the dim, all I could think about were the angry faces in the window.

The next morning was the Sabbath. Rabbi led the seven of us through the croplands outside the city, to the synagogue. Olives, chickpeas, cucumbers, melons, and wheat were ripe for the picking. I strummed my hand along the tips of grain. Dry stalks tickled my shin as I trekked close behind Him. Deciding things were more dangerous meant staying close. Nathanael and James grabbed the wheat and ate it, but Rabbi didn't stop them—and we all started picking our favorites.

It was forbidden, but I couldn't help myself. I wrapped my hand around a cucumber and plucked it, careful to watch the edge of the field. My eyes met Zedekiah's arched eyebrow. Behind him, Shet spit on the ground. More leaders came, snarling at the others as they joyfully grabbed foods that we hadn't eaten in months.

As we made our way past them, Zedekiah grabbed Peter and Andrew's sacks. "I've had enough of this so-called Rabbi! Look, they labor on the Sabbath, collecting grain," he shouted shuffling through Peter's bounty. He handed it to the other leaders.

"Their mouths are full," Shet added as he circled our group. "Why? Did You not teach Your talmidim the law?" He stopped in front of Rabbi. "All of you see here, their sacks are full!"

Those heading to the synagogue stopped and came our way.

Zedekiah demanded, "Your disciples are breaking the Sabbath rules! Work six days, but the seventh day will be a holy rest day, God's holy rest day. Anyone who works on this day must be put to death."

All I could do was take in the number of people and count the stones on the ground that were heavy enough to kill with a single throw.

Rabbi looked at Zedekiah. "Really? Haven't you ever read what David did when he was hungry, along with those who were with him? How he entered the sanctuary and ate fresh bread off the altar, with the chief priest, Abiathar, right there watching—holy bread that no one but priests were allowed to eat—and handed it out to his companions?"

Everyone knows the story. King David ruled as God's anointed. A warrior, slaying tens of thousands of enemy forces, was betrayed by his jealous predecessor, King Saul, and removed from his post as commander. Pursued to the point of starvation, David and his men were forced into the sanctuary of the synagogue. However, the high priest allowed David to eat the holy showbread, reserved by law for the priests themselves. David ate and shared it with the others. For generations, he's been celebrated for his determination under persecution.

Silence. No one dared challenge Rabbi's point, but then He said, "There is far more at stake here than religion. If you had any idea what this scripture meant— 'I prefer a flexible heart to an inflexible ritual'—you wouldn't be nitpicking like this. The Sabbath was made to serve us; we weren't made to serve the Sabbath. The Son of Man is no lackey to the Sabbath. He's in charge!"

I sucked in a breath and held it. Balling my fists, I readied for the first stone. The leaders had what they needed, but Rabbi just turned and walked to the temple.

We began to follow.

"It is enough!" Zedekiah shouted at our backs. "It is one thing to lead the young astray. And another to perform deceptions and illusions for the public, but now He places Himself above our law, in line with God!"

I turned around, watching as he paced back and forth outside the synagogue. Rabbi stood near the door, greeting the people.

"I will take no more humiliation. I cannot allow this Deceiver to go on stealing the innocence of young men, robbing our citizens of the truth. He must be silenced!" Zedekiah said, shaking his fist through the air. "It is our duty!"

Rabbi ignored his words and went inside, but I couldn't follow. I needed to know if the others agreed. Lingering behind, I heard Shet ask, "What can we do? He threatens the teachings, but at the same time, He embodies it."

Zedekiah said, "We will dispose of Him the way we have done before. We will turn to those ahead of us and consult the heads of the synagogue in Jerusalem. They will put a stop to this insolence and depravity, but we must leave now. Shet and I will go and inform the high priest. The rest of you remain here and guard the teachings from this Agitator. I expect a full report of His blasphemies and corruptions."

"Yes, we need evidence to convict this Jesus—and more than

one person's testimony of wrongdoings. Our own infuriation will not be enough," Shet instructed. "Hezekiah, you and your men, follow Him and His talmidim. See what they do. We will put an end to this."

Zedekiah and Shet turned around, leaving the other leaders in the street.

"Jesus must die," Zedekiah shouted, glaring back at me.

My mouth hung open. Catching myself, I hurried inside.

CHAPTER NINE

the twelve

Spring rains filled the wadis, changing them from our paths into raging rivers. Thunder and lightning crashed, and we hid up high. I held my cloak above my head, looking down from the edge of the road into the chaos. The leaders were like the water at the base of the valley—uncontrolled and destroying everything—and they were coming.

When the rain slowed, we huddled around each other and wrung out our things. I knelt down, filling my pouch. A single purple carmelite flower survived, poking through the rocks. Plucking it, I twisted it between two fingers, thinking about my dream from the night before. It was the opposite of a nightmare, not unlike the beauty of the flower. I saw a gold menorah with seven branches and in the center, the Son of Man, in a robe and gold breastplate, hair a blizzard of white. Eyes pouring fire-blaze, both feet furnace-fired bronze.

But what did it mean?

"What's the matter, John?" James asked, crouching beside me. Before I could answer, he said, "The leaders are coming. Did you see the man following us? I recognize him from the temple in Jerusalem."

"Yes."

He raised his eyebrows. "They must have gone to the high priest. If he hears Rabbi speak—"

"Rabbi cannot stop His message any more than the Baptizer could. We can protect Him," I interrupted, standing up.

"Can we?" He stood and looked me in the eye. "Like you protected the Baptizer?"

I looked away. "The only thing we can do is wait."

"That's what everyone keeps saying."

"I don't like waiting for an ambush any more than you do, but for now, there's no other way. We need time to figure out what everything means."

"Everything?"

"There's more than what you see. Something else is working here."

"What else?"

"Something … dark."

"Dark?"

"Yes, or worse than dark. Something fed by it. Something hidden."

"John, is this about your dreams again?"

"No ... I mean, yes, but it's more than that. The leaders can't be stopped. They're misguided, confused about the truth, being told lies."

"Lies by whom?"

"I don't know if they'll ever understand," I said.

"Maybe you're right," he said.

Rabbi gestured for us to follow Him down the hillside toward the lake. We did. The crowd came with the sunlight as it broke through the clouds. Before long, hundreds pressed our group into the lake's edge. Rabbi moved through them with a huge grin, surveying them.

He came to James and me. Pointing into the distance, He told us to get a boat propped on the shore. As we walked, James laughed to himself. "Remember when we saw Him teaching on the boat?"

I gave a half smile. "I've never swam so fast in my life."

"Things are so different now. Would you leave again, knowing what you know now?"

"I would."

"Me too." He grabbed the edge of the boat, pulling it free from the rocks. "John, I don't what you mean—or what's happening—but I'm here for you. You know that?"

"I do." I took the other side, and we dragged it along.

When we returned, Rabbi got inside, and we pushed Him out a few feet in the water to keep the people from trampling Him. Looking at them, I could see different walks of life, young and old. They came from Judea, Jerusalem, Idumea, and the regions across the Jordan and around Tyre and Sidon. I'd never seen such diversity—or seen Rabbi so still.

He knows something. Why doesn't He teach?

Rabbi called out the name Simon and gestured to Peter. Peter moved through the crowd and stood next to Him with a broad smile. Then, He gave him the name Peter, but this time for the people to hear. He called James and me, giving us the name *Boanerges*, which meant "sons of thunder." I liked the name, but I didn't know what was happening.

He called Andrew, Philip, Nathanael, and Matthew—and then the names, James, Thomas, Thaddaeus, Simon, and Judas Iscariot. Among the people, they stepped forward and came to the shore. I looked at their faces. Rabbi flung Himself over the boat's edge into the shallow water. He walked up to the crowd and began speaking with the people.

The twelve of us stood there. Peter spoke, breaking the awkward silence. "As you heard, I'm Peter, and this is my brother Andrew. And these two are the 'sons of thunder,'" he said, pointing.

"Brothers? We're brothers too," one interjected, pushing a tall, pale boy. "Thaddeus and me. I'm James, son of Alpheus. You're Zebedee's sons?" he said with flashing eyes.

I glared at Thaddeus's pristine sandals and careful clothes, a difficult thing considering the rain. Everything about him was ordered. Even his hair was parted perfectly down the center of his head, and the leather satchel slung across his shoulder looked new. James was his opposite, short and dirty. They barely looked related. "Shalom," I greeted them.

Thaddeus stared at me like he wanted to punch me in the face.

"Don't mind him. He doesn't talk much, which is odd because I'm younger, but only by two years. And don't mind his look. He's always clean, needs to be. He's always been that way. Any other state makes him upset, so I wouldn't mess with him. Did I mention my name was James? You can call me James. All my friends do."

"Friends?" another said with a curled lip.

"And you are?" I asked.

"Judas."

The new James cocked his head. "What's wrong with saying *friend*?"

"Odd thing to say to people you've just met." He stared at

the others with dark eyes under bushy black eyebrows. "Is it that simple?" He stroked his pointy chin with bony fingers.

"We don't have to be friends, but we need to get along," Andrew replied.

Judas raised an eyebrow, gripping his bag as if he were about to be robbed. "What's your problem?" I asked.

"I don't have one."

"You *are* among friends," Peter said. "We have traveled with each other for some time, as brothers do."

Another pushed forward. "A brotherhood? I like the sound of that. I'm Simon. I've heard whispers of your group from the leaders," he said, bouncing his eyebrows. "They call you a rebellion. Of course, with Rabbi adding the rest of us, it'll make them angrier." He moved closer and whispered, "I'm a Zealot, so this is perfect for me."

A radical. Just what we need—some rioter trying to attack the Romans with a handmade sword.

"You won't need any of your previous skills in this group," Peter said. "We do not seek trouble. We avoid it."

Simon crossed muscular arms across his chest. "Do you? I've been tracking this group for months, and all I've heard is trouble. I mean, I have powerful ideas for a fourteen-year-old, which I usually channel into rage and discourse, so I've been told, but I've never heard anything like what Rabbi preaches."

"Where are you from?" Nathanael asked, scowling.

"No roots in any particular city. I travel with other the Zealots."

"To where?" James demanded.

"Wherever. Different places."

"Where are your parents?" Philip asked with a concerned look.

"Don't know. Don't have any."

Judas said, "You don't have parents?"

"Doesn't matter. Why all the questions? You all sound like a bunch of spies for the filthy Romans."

"What? No, how could we be here if we were?" I was getting irritated.

"Not sure why you're here, but the Messiah is supposed to fight for the people's freedom with bloodshed."

"He doesn't do that," Peter said.

"Well, I know that. I never imagined He would come uncovering the mysteries of God. It's more than I could hope for, but eventually He will purify our faith. Extract the Roman hogs!"

"Anyone else?" Peter said, turning to the others.

"Good thing He changed your name to Peter—or that would be confusing," Simon said, punching his arm. He swung another strong slap at Peter's upper arm, tossing his unruly curls out of his line of sight. "Don't worry. I know you're in charge, so I won't challenge you on who's the better Simon," he said with a laugh.

Peter sighed. "This is Philip, Nathanael, and Matthew," he said.

"I'm not sure why we need more talmidim, and certainly not the ones in the circle," James added. "And we'll have to figure out what to call you, son of Alphaeus. I'm not changing my name."

"James, how old are you?" Peter asked.

"Fourteen, fifteen soon," he answered.

"According to tradition, since James, son of Zebedee, is fifteen, we will call you James the lesser," Peter instructed.

"Works for me," James said, winking at James the lesser.

"And you?" Philip asked.

"Thomas," he answered. "Is this it?" he asked, "Do you all just wait around, talking? And don't you think it's odd to be called by a rabbi when none of you work in the temple?"

"Rabbi has good reason for His choice, including you," Andrew answered.

Thomas took off his round hat and scratched his blond hair. He glared doubtfully with blue eyes. "I understand that, but I'm only fourteen—and the rest of you are a bunch of kids. No wonder the leaders are so upset."

"Thomas, you'll see what Rabbi can do. Don't worry," Philip answered.

Peter looked at the group. "Let's find Rabbi," he instructed.

Before we could move, Rabbi came and took the twelve of us back toward town.

The twelve. A brotherhood. Not the sort Simon bragged about. Smart, less dangerous—chosen.

We stopped in front of a wooden door. I hadn't been there in so long. The careful carving of a weathered tree was unmistakable, unlike any other in town. I fit my finger inside a knot at its center, waiting for the others.

Rabbi took the new boys to the market to gather food for our meal. The rest of us waited outside. I could see Him at the end of the street. He cocked His head at our waiting. Maybe He expected us to go in, but the uncertainty of our days made us wonder who was on the other side.

Soon we were in the main room where a cold breeze from the courtyard carried the scent of sizzling fish, cumin, and fennel. My head swung behind me at the door. It shook.

"Who is it now?" James said, turning to the noise.

"We are here for your rabbi!" a muffled voice shouted.

James looked at me. "Should we open it?"

Down the hall, the door to the alleyway shook.

"Go tell Rabbi," I demanded, running to the front. Slamming into the door, I held it closed. "Whoever it is, they aren't waiting for an invitation. Hurry."

"They wouldn't try to pry the door open … would they?"

"Brother, do you really want to find out? They'll arrest you too. Get the others!" I yanked my head in their direction.

He ran and veered midway down the hallway, to the courtyard. "Rabbi! Peter—"

Planting my feet apart, I refused to let whoever it was in, but the clanking at the back door grew more desperate. It broke free, and light pierced the black hallway. I took off. Before I could reach it, a hand wrapped around the edge of the door. "Who are you?" I hollered, stopping short.

Wide-eyed, a tiny man answered, "You are His talmid." He trembled.

I'd be in trouble if I hurt him.

He turned behind him. "We are at the right home! Come see," he said.

Where is James?

The man waved inward, and a flood of people rushed inside, pressing me against the wall.

"John? Where are you?" James shouted, but it was too late.

"I'm here!" I answered, pushing through.

Someone grabbed my arm. "You there. You're Jesus's talmid. I've seen you with Him." Behind him, I saw more eager eyes.

"I am," I answered.

"John! I haven't seen you in some time. Jude, let go of his arm. You're scaring him."

"Yes, Mother."

"Where is my Son?" she asked.

"The courtyard." I pointed.

I led them to Rabbi, but there was little room to move. "We've come from Nazareth." A girl with eyes like blades of grass held her palms together. She was about to burst. "We've heard the news! His miracles, is it all true?" she asked.

I nodded.

"I've never heard Him teach," Jude said with his chin up. "Finally, we can see why He is worthy of such admiration."

"Jealous." She smirked. "Sister, can you believe it? Our own Brother, *the Messiah*."

"We will see," she answered. She was older than me, but younger than her brothers. Scratching her forearm, she tucked her curls behind her ear.

"You've heard the stories. The leaders are enraged by His words." Jude touched his thick brown beard. He pulled his shawl over his shoulder-length hair. He looked like Rabbi, but a bit different. "We need to be careful not to be seen. Before they think we, as His family, are the same."

"We need to take Him back to Nazareth before they stone Him—by force if necessary."

"Justus, do you really think the leaders will hurt Him," the youngest asked, deferring to a tall, lanky man.

"I don't know, but Jude is right. His might be our big Brother, but we need to be careful."

Mary shook her head gently. "Come," she said. "He's over there." She pointed at Rabbi. "It's been months since we've seen Him. His ministry is of the utmost importance, and it will continue whether you all accept it or not."

Jude said, "Surely no man is this important. Let us see why Your name is on every lip in Nazareth and beyond."

"This way," I said, pointing to an opening along the wall.

We squeezed through and made it as far as we could. Standing outside the courtyard, Mary adjusted her dark veil. "Thank you, John. This will do." As soon as she saw Him, tears ran down her round face. She smiled from ear to ear, but His sisters and brothers looked confused as Rabbi began to teach.

Jude crossed his arms and pressed his brows to the center of his face. "He's crazy!" he shouted, interrupting Rabbi.

Traitor. You're His brother.

The room was quiet. All eyes were on Jude. It seemed like the thing he wanted in the first place.

Then I saw them. Shet and Zedekiah. They were back, standing among the crowd.

Shet said, "See here? His own family accuses Him."

"Shet, wait. Let Josephus be the one to speak on behalf of the high priest," Zedekiah said.

The high priest?

A man stood wobbling. A strong wind would be enough to knock him over, but I knew the older they were, the more versed he would be. "He is using black magic! Using demon tricks to impress you," he shouted. "He is far too young to know the teachings as He does. It has taken many of us almost forty years to learn, yet He recites it with the ease of a demon."

Lies.

I wanted to say something, but it wasn't my place. Meanwhile, His family stood silent.

Rabbi looked at them. "Does it make sense to send a devil to catch a devil, to use Satan to get rid of Satan? A constantly squabbling family disintegrates. If Satan were fighting Satan, there soon wouldn't be any Satan left. But if it's by God's power that I am sending the evil spirits packing, then God's kingdom is here for sure. How in the world do you think it's possible in broad daylight to enter the house of an awake, able-bodied man and walk off with his possessions unless you tie him up first? Tie him up, though, and you can clean him out. This is war, and there is no neutral ground. If you're not on My side, you're the enemy; if you're not helping, you're making things worse."

The war from my dream.

"Listen to this carefully. I'm warning you. There's nothing done or said that can't be forgiven, but if you persist in your slanders against God's Holy Spirit, you are repudiating the very One who forgives, sawing off the branch on which you're sitting, severing by your own perversity all connection with the One who forgives."

Jude shoved a man in front of us. "Tell my brother I need a word with Him." He turned and looked at Jude, and then he whispered to a man in front of him. Word spread forward until it reached Rabbi.

"Who do you think are My mother and brothers?" Looking around, Rabbi said, "Right here, right in front of you, My mother and My brothers. Obedience is thicker than blood. The person who obeys God's will is My brother and sister and mother."

Justus and Jude groaned and mumbled to themselves, but my eyes turned to the leaders as they made their way out of Rabbi's home.

A good thing I wasn't at His side. I moved to the door just as the leaders stepped outside. My heart beat through my chest, and I pressed my ear against a break in the wood of the door.

"Josephus, you see now what odds are against us. The people will not listen to reason," Zedekiah shouted.

"Yes, it is far worse than I imagined. Calling Oneself God? This cannot stand! This Deceiver blasphemes with no regard for the teachings." Josephus paced shakily back and forth.

I pressed harder as a bead of sweat dripped down my cheek.

"We must go to Caiaphas. The matter is beyond our own efforts," Josephus said, scowling at the door.

I dropped down, hoping he couldn't see my eye in the hole.

Josephus said, "These wayward lambs, who have become His people, must be redirected—lest they be thrown into a pit of fire and damnation. Those in and around this home are playing ear to dangerous teachings and losing their grip on reality. We know it is dark forces that empower this Jesus, giving Him knowledge and the power to heal. We are the only ones who can stop Him. He has to die! This infection has spread far enough, but we can stop it if we act quickly. We need only involve the high priest. I have watched him snuff out disruptions in the past."

I ran back, pushing and shoving my way through. Just as I made it, Rabbi called my name and the rest of the twelve and said, "Don't begin by traveling to some far-off place to convert unbelievers. And don't try to be dramatic by tackling some public enemy. Go to the lost, confused people right here in the neighborhood. Tell them that the kingdom is here. Bring health to the sick. Raise the dead. Touch the untouchables. Kick out the demons. You have been treated generously, so live generously."

Wait. What? I can't leave. Not now.

Walking, He placed both hands on each of our shoulders. We looked at each other.

"How will we take care of ourselves? Should we seek work?" Judas asked.

He responded, "Don't think you have to put on a fund-raising campaign before you start. You don't need a lot of equipment. You are the equipment—and all you need to keep that going is three meals a day. Travel light."

"So how will we afford a place to sleep? Do we come back here each night?" Thomas asked.

"When you enter a town or village, don't insist on staying in a luxury inn. Get a modest place with some modest people—and be content there until you leave. When you knock on a door, be courteous in your greeting. If they welcome you, be gentle in your conversation. If they don't welcome you, quietly withdraw. Don't make a scene. Shrug your shoulders and be on your way. You can be sure that they'll be mighty sorry on Judgment Day, but it's no concern of yours now."

"Rabbi, most of us are new. How can we deliver Your words on our own?" James the lesser asked, scratching his head.

"Our age will only make it more difficult for people to take us seriously," Judas said.

"The leaders were here. They were upset with all that was said." Matthew looked at Him. "I don't think I am ready to face my own enemies with, I'm sorry to say it, an unpopular message. How is that safe?"

"Stay alert. This is hazardous work I'm assigning you. You're going to be like sheep running through a wolf pack, so don't call attention to yourselves. Be as cunning as a snake, inoffensive as a dove. Don't be naive. Some people will impugn your motives, and others will smear your reputation—just because you believe in Me. Don't be upset when they haul you before the civil authorities. Without knowing it, they've done you—and Me—a favor, given you a platform for preaching the kingdom news!"

"Authorities?" James said, wide-eyed. "Rabbi, we are not ready to face the leaders. No one is going to listen to me about anything."

How will we know what to say?

"And don't worry about what you'll say or how you'll say it. The right words will be there; the Spirit of your Father will supply the words."

James continued, "And what will our families say of our arrests?"

"My brothers will be with me! We've been through worse!" Simon shouted. "I'm used to causing an uproar and welcome the chance to do something dangerous."

"Brothers? I thought you had no family." Judas shook his head.

"When people realize it is the living God you are presenting and not some idol that makes them feel good, they are going to turn on you—even people in your own family. There is a great irony here: proclaiming so much love, experiencing so much hate! But don't quit. Don't cave in. It is all well worth it in the end. It is not success you are after in such times but survival. Be survivors! Before you've run out of options, the Son of Man will have arrived."

"But You are here now, Rabbi," Andrew said.

Everyone grew silent.

I wanted to blurt out like the others, but my concern wasn't for myself.

"Rabbi, we are *not* ready," James maintained.

"A student doesn't get a better desk than her teacher. A laborer doesn't make more money than his boss. Be content—pleased, even—when you, My students, My harvest hands, get the same treatment I get. If they call Me, the Master, 'Dungface,' what can the workers expect?

"Don't be intimidated. Eventually everything is going to be out in the open, and everyone will know how things really are. So don't hesitate to go public now."

He bowed His head and prayed, "Stand up for Me against world opinion, and I'll stand up for you before My Father in heaven. If you turn tail and run, do you think I'll cover for you? We are intimately linked in this harvest work. Anyone who accepts what you do, accepts Me, the One who sent you. Anyone who accepts what I do accepts My Father, who sent Me."

I hung on His every word, worried it was my last with Him.

Then He left out the back door.

Peter looked at us. He paused, silent, while the moments blurred. "Rabbi has gone to teach in other towns. We will split up and do the same."

"Split up? Why? That's dangerous, considering the odds against us," Thomas said.

"We will draw less attention from the leaders if we are in smaller groups. Rabbi is trusting us with His message. So we need to act as He would, say what He would. I know many of you are new, and not sure what to say or do, but as Rabbi explained, the word will be given to you."

CHAPTER TEN

five thousand

The next morning, a few of us were still in His home. I put on my tunic, went to the courtyard, and stared through the empty house. *I thought I could trust this choice, Rabbi, but I'm lost.*

"I'm glad you're in my group, John," Andrew said, stepping into the courtyard. "I wasn't sure how we would get along without Peter, but I think the other talmidim need him more."

I didn't say anything.

Andrew bent over and warmed bread on a stone near the flames. "I'm going inside to grab cheese." When he returned, he said, "John, you know the teachings better than any of us. We will need your insight if we are going to preach to the people." He popped a piece of bread into his mouth. "Where's James?"

"Still sleeping. I'll go get him." I walked to the room where we had slept, but James was gone. Walking through the house, I called, "James, where are you?"

No answer.

I went to the back door and opened it. There he was. "What are you doing? We need to head to the marketplace. It's our best chance to find people."

He sighed loudly and came inside without a word.

There was an uncomfortable silence as we collected our things. It wasn't long before we closed the door behind us.

"How do we draw a crowd?" Andrew asked.

James stood at the door.

"Come on, James," Andrew said.

"What are you doing, brother?" I asked, staring at his hand on the door. He looked past us and out to the street.

"We haven't obeyed Rabbi's instructions. Waiting here accomplishes nothing for the kingdom of God," Andrew added.

"James," I said, "remember what Rabbi promised? It will work." Nothing.

"Brother, what's the matter?"

"What's he doing?" Andrew whispered to me. "We don't have time for this." He looked at James. "Of all the times to stop running your mouth, you choose now?"

"Relax, Andrew," I said, knowing it wasn't the time to get him mad.

James clutched his temples with both hands. "We have no idea what we are doing! We can't do it! I can't remember anything from the scrolls. How will I outwit the Pharisees in town as Rabbi does? I don't want to end up like the Baptizer, trapped in a dark prison."

"We haven't even started yet; how can you be so sure we'll be arrested?" Andrew asked.

"You're fine. Come on." I said, holding out my hand.

He leaned the back of his head on the door. "We could walk out here and be stoned to death!" he shouted. "Do you want to have rocks pelted at you until you die?"

Andrew and I looked at each other. We knew the risks, but having them said out loud was unnerving.

James cleared his throat. "Look, I want to recite scripture as Rabbi does, but I can't remember anything. Don't you see this is madness?"

"I've had enough! You know what I see?" Andrew walked eye to chin with him. "A coward!"

Andrew, don't.

"Disbelief! You lack confidence in yourself, and worse, you lack confidence in God. You think this is about what you can do? What you're capable of? It's not! Not everything is about your doubt and self-pity!" Andrew balled his fists as the words left his mouth.

"Back off," James said, letting go of the door.

"James, Rabbi has shown each of us so much—and now it's our turn to use it. You have to be willing to try," I said, trying to encourage him.

"Try to get myself killed?"

"Let's go now!" Andrew said through clenched teeth. "Don't you see God can use you—even if you aren't enough? He can fill in all the holes and make you complete. He can even speak for you!"

"Get out of my face!" James shoved Andrew to the ground.

Andrew stood up. "You're wasting time. What will you say of yourself when Peter finds out we did nothing? What will you do if we run into Rabbi? What then? Tell Him we couldn't do anything that He showed us? Is that what we should do, James?"

"Stop! We can't fight among ourselves. There is enough waiting for us on the other side of this street!" I said, gripping James's arm.

"Say one more word," he demanded. "All you care about is disappointing Peter, not Rabbi. You're no more sure than I am."

"You're not listening. This is not about you. Or who you think will find out. We need—"

James lunged at Andrew, pushed to the ground, sat on Andrew's chest, and swung fist after fist at his face.

Andrew swung back, while trying to protect his face with his other hand.

I placed both arms around James's waist and lifted him up in one swift motion.

"He thinks he knows everything!" James shouted.

Andrew put his arms behind him and lifted himself to a seated position. His nose and lip were bleeding. "Look what you did." He touched his lips and winced. "Now we can't go into town. You've ruined everything. Everyone will know you hit me, and Rabbi will look like He called a bunch of criminals to speak the message of God!"

"You have a bloody nose, and your concern is how to cover it up? Are you serious?" James said, barely making eye contact with the damage he had caused.

"Enough!" I ordered. "What's happening here? You two haven't spoken an unkind word to each other in months—and now you want to punch each other? We are cowards, afraid to walk into the town we grew up in and share a message we believe in. A message we know will change their lives. What's worse is we will have to explain our lack of obedience to Rabbi."

James stared at the ground. "I messed up. Rabbi trusted me, and all I've done is complain. He saved my life from pointlessness, and I'm not going to go back to it." He reached into his sack, grabbed a piece of cloth, and tossed it to Andrew. "I'm sorry, but we can't worry about what this looks like. We have to move on. That means sharing what we've learned no matter what." He looked up at us. "Unless you two are ready to go home?"

"Never," I said.

"No," Andrew answered, wiping his face.

"Good. Then let's go. You're both right. Yes, we're young, but so is Rabbi compared to the other rabbis and prophets. He does it—and so can we. We just need faith." He extended his hand and helped Andrew to his feet.

"I'm sorry too." Andrew poured water from his animal skin pouch onto the cloth and cleaned his face.

Months later, we reunited with Rabbi. Gathered on a hill around Him, the twelve reported what we had done and taught. Time concealed James and Andrew's fight, and the three of us decided not to discuss our start. It was difficult traveling on rough paths and speaking for ourselves to disinterested people who felt awkward at the mention of His name, confused new recruits messing up the message before we reached a certain town, and leaders ready to combat our every word. It was right to be at His side again.

He said, "Come off by yourselves; let's take a break and get a little rest."

So we went away by boat, heading to a solitary place, north of the sea to Bethsaida.

A man at the shore saw us leaving. "It's Him!" he shouted, pointing. He must have run on foot like a maniac to all the towns because they got to the other side ahead of us.

When we landed, Rabbi saw the large crowd. It looked like His heart was breaking; they were like sheep with no shepherd. He went right to work teaching them.

The twelve stood listening to how it was really done.

A group of men interrupted Him, asking to talk. Moments

later, Rabbi shared the news with Peter. Peter's chin trembled at His words.

What's happening?

Rabbi stepped away and talked with the men.

Peter looked over to Andrew and me.

My hands began to sweat. "John, Andrew, come here."

We parted from the twelve and walked to where Peter was at the front of the crowd. "You both know King Herod had arrested and imprisoned the Baptizer as a favor to his wife Herodias, his brother Philip's wife?"

I bit the inside of my lip, remembering Abba's warning.

"John had provoked Herod by naming his relationship with Herodias 'adultery.'"

James looked at my face and walked over. "What's going on?"

"He's talking about the Baptizer," Andrew answered, biting his nail.

"Peter, our father told us that Herodias nursed a grudge against the Baptizer and wanted to kill him since he threatened her status. We aren't supposed to talk about it."

Seconds later, the rest of the twelve came.

"What is it now?" Judas asked, brows toward his nose.

"The Baptizer," Peter offered. "Herod wanted to kill him, but he was afraid because so many people revered John as a prophet of God."

"So what?" Philip asked.

Peter looked at him. "Herodias, smoldering with hate, wanted to kill him, but didn't dare because Herod was in awe of John."

Simon stepped forward. "I traveled with a group who knew the inside of the prison."

"So?" Philip asked.

"So I was told the king was—" he leaned in, "convinced that he was a holy man, he gave him special treatment. Whenever he listened to him, he was miserable with guilt—and yet he couldn't stay away. Something in John kept pulling him back."

Peter looked at them. "Stop interrupting. Just listen!" He collected himself. "Herodias found her opportunity ..."

"What happened?" I asked, pushing past the others.

"Herod threw a birthday party, inviting all the brass and bluebloods in Galilee. Herodias's daughter entered the banquet hall and danced for the guests. She dazzled Herod and the guests."

Thomas tossed his hands up. "What does that have to do with the Baptizer?"

"The king said to the girl, 'Ask me anything. I'll give you anything you want.' Carried away, he kept on, 'I swear, I'll split my kingdom with you if you say so!' She went back to her mother and said, 'What should I ask for?'

"'Ask for the head of John the Baptizer.'

"Excited, she ran back to the king and said, 'I want the head of John the Baptizer served up on a platter. And I want it now!'"

James said, "Surely the king would not cater to some brat because she danced for him?"

"Unwilling to lose face with his guests, he caved in and let her have her wish."

"Not possible!" Andrew said.

"The king sent the executioner off to the prison with orders to bring back John's head. He went, cut off John's head, brought it back on a platter, and presented it to the girl, who gave it to her mother."

No!

Everything went black. I could see the river where we stood together, where I waited for him, but it was empty. The water was flat and smooth, motionless. Something stirred it, and something glided across it. A shadow rose from the water and grinned. I shook and shook and shook—

"John. John. John wake up! John are you okay!" my brother asked in a shaking voice.

I woke to His face, held by the Savior, Healer, Demon chaser— but I was broken, lost, afraid. "I should have been there. I could have done more to help, and now it's too late," I muttered to Him.

"No one in history surpasses John the Baptizer, but in the kingdom he prepared you for, the lowliest person is ahead of him. For a long time now, people have tried to force themselves into God's kingdom, but if you read the books of the prophets and God's Law closely, you will see them culminate in John, teaming up with him in preparing the way for the Messiah of the kingdom. Looked at in this way, John is the 'Elijah' you've all been expecting to arrive and introduce the Messiah.

"How can I account for this generation? The people have been like spoiled children whining to their parents, 'We wanted to skip rope, and you were always too tired; we wanted to talk, but you were always too busy.' John came fasting, and they called him crazy. I came feasting, and they called me a lush, a friend of the riffraff. Opinion polls don't count for much, do they? The proof of the pudding is in the eating."

I tried to be calm, but images of the Baptizer alone in a dark prison awaiting his cruel fate filled my mind. Looking at Rabbi, I knew I should have told Him—warned Him even. Maybe there was something I could have done. The questions were too much. A bubble expanded in my stomach, lifting my food to my throat. I tried to swallow the chunks, but more came. I couldn't hold it. My body flung to my side, and I lost everything inside me.

Rabbi embraced me more firmly, patting me on my back as if He wanted me to get it all out. All of it. All the hate, anger, and frustration of being lost, being afraid, confused, the burden of my dreams—it felt like he was pouring them onto the floor with my lost supper in a stew of undigested lies. Every upchuck forced me to live in the current moment and accept that the Baptizer was already gone.

Tears in His eyes, He said, "Doom to you, Chorazin! Doom, Bethsaida! If Tyre and Sidon had seen half of the powerful miracles you have seen, they would have been on their knees in a minute. At Judgment Day, they'll get off easy compared to you. And Capernaum! With all your peacock strutting, you are going to end up in the abyss. If the people of Sodom had had your chances, the city would still be around. At Judgment Day, they'll get off easy compared to you ..."

"Thank you, Father, Lord of heaven and earth. You've concealed your ways from sophisticates and know-it-alls—but spelled them out clearly to ordinary people. Yes, Father, that's the way you like to work."

"The Father has given Me all these things to do and say. This is a unique Father-Son operation, coming out of Father-and-Son intimacies and knowledge. No one knows the Son the way the Father does, nor the Father the way the Son does, but I'm not keeping it to Myself; I'm ready to go over it line by line with anyone willing to listen."

He was upset. We grieved together. I sighed, releasing my guilt with a single breath. *But where do I go from here?*

Rabbi helped me sit up, staying close. He wiped my face on His sleeve and lifted my sweaty curls from my forehead.

I felt weak.

He placed His hands over my heart and said, "Are you tired? Worn out? Burned out on religion? Come to Me. Get away with Me, and you'll recover your life. I'll show you how to take a real rest. Walk with Me and work with Me—watch how I do it. Learn the unforced rhythms of grace. I won't lay anything heavy or ill-fitting on you. Keep company with Me, and you'll learn to live freely and lightly."

He chose me. Rabbi needs me. He's my friend, and I will protect Him. I have to—no matter what. I won't make the same mistake.

I looked around, gaining sense of my surroundings. Hundreds waited at the river's edge for Rabbi, but He postponed it to speak with me.

"Thank you, Rabbi."

He bowed His head. I had seen Him using every moment to be gentle and humble toward every ailment, heartache, illness, leaving His self behind.

As I sat there surrounded by everyone, holding up the journey and Rabbi teaching, I wanted to be grateful—to be like Him. In that moment, I was being anything but. I stood up, shook the dirt from my clothes, and joined the others in front of the crowd.

Rabbi rose. He welcomed the people, spoke to them about the kingdom of God, and healed those who needed healing.

In the evening, Peter came to Him. "We're out in the country, and it's getting late. Dismiss the people so they can go to the villages and get some supper."

"There is no need to dismiss them. You give them supper."

Rabbi asked Philip, "Where can we buy bread to feed these people?"

"Two hundred silver pieces wouldn't be enough to buy bread for each person to get a piece."

Judas agreed, clutching his money bag. "Are you serious? You want us to go spend a fortune on food for their supper?"

He was quite serious. "How many loaves of bread do you have? Take an inventory."

Peter looked at us, "We will go and find out who has food and is willing to give it to Rabbi."

"Who would give away their food?" Thomas asked.

Judas crossed his arms. "This isn't going to work. I wouldn't give my money to these people, so how could I ask it of them? I'm not asking anyone anything."

"Why should you be allowed to disrespect Rabbi?" I asked, moving toward him.

Andrew placed his hand on my shoulder. "Ignore him. Surely someone here believes and will be generous. We'll ask together."

"No, my brother is right," James said. "Rabbi has given enough of His time. The very least these people can do is give back."

"No one owes us anything," I held. "We can't move through

the crowd demanding anything outside generosity. No one has to give, James."

James huffed. "Fine." He made his own path through the crowd.

"John, over there." Andrew was pointing to a family sitting in a circle a few feet away. "Let's ask them. The woman has a kind face; surely, she will have pity on us. They have a travel sack. There must be food in it."

"Good idea."

We walked over to a woman on the ground holding her daughter.

"Excuse us. Do you have any bread or fish?" Andrew asked.

She looked up at us and said nothing.

"Is there anything you can give?" I asked.

"We've come a long way, and we're not wealthy. What we have is enough for us alone," she answered, looking away.

Andrew turned to me. "How can they refuse? We're far from home too. We're only here to spread the truth to people like them, and all they can do is say no? What about us?"

"It's for Rabbi, not us," I answered, not sure what to do next. I looked out to the other talmidim in the distance who were being shunned or ignored.

"Look at the others. No one is giving," Andrew said with a sigh.

"We just have to—"

"You can have my food."

I looked down at a boy, holding up his sack. "It's not much, but maybe your Rabbi can use it." I crouched in front of him. He was five or so, with no family nearby. He smiled with a soiled face and tattered tunic.

"He's your Rabbi too." I smiled at him.

"Will it be enough?" he asked, unwrapping five small barley loaves and two fish from a piece of cloth. "I didn't eat. I was listening to *our* Rabbi teach." He grinned.

"Let's get it to Rabbi. Thank you," Andrew said.

I stood up. "Thank you."

We moved through the crowd, back to the others and Rabbi.

Andrew said, "There's a little boy here who has five barley loaves and two fish, but that's a drop in the bucket for a crowd like this."

"Bring them here. Make the people sit down."

He instructed us to have the people sit down in groups of about fifty each in the soft grass.

Peter stood before the crowd and shouted, "Sit, please! Everyone, take a seat."

So many. Thousands.

I sat down between Andrew and James.

"We don't have enough to feed everyone," James whispered.

"There have to be fifteen thousand people here," Andrew said. "I've never seen this many people gather outside the synagogue."

"Thousands to five loaves of bread," James said.

I was enamored by the volume quietly waiting on Rabbi. He took the loaves, raised them above His head, gave thanks to God, and handed one to Peter seated at His side—then another and another.

I passed a loaf to Andrew, then a second loaf, and soon a tenth. "The boy only handed you five, right Andrew?" James asked.

"Yes."

Another and another passed among the people. I studied one in my hand. There was nothing supernatural about it. I tore it … more bread inside. *How can this be?*

Rabbi raised the fish, gave thanks, and passed it to Peter. The aroma of fish filled the night air as people began feasting on the abundance. I watched in awe as thousands ate their fill. Families handed pieces to their children and their neighbors, smiling and laughing in thanks of God's provision.

I took a piece of fish and ate. Hungry, I chased it down with bread, filling my sore stomach.

Andrew passed me more, and I happily received and ate. It was the first time in a long time in forever I felt full. I tore more pieces of bread, filling my mouth, and leaned over to James. "This is the best bread I've ever eaten," I said, spitting out bits of bread with every syllable.

"What do you expect of bread from heaven and fish held by the Son of God," James asked.

Andrew sipped water from his animal skin pouch, wiping his mouth. "It's a miracle! All these people eating their fill. Though I don't understand how it happened."

James the lesser scooted along the grass to us. "This is so crazy. I'm dreaming." He rolled a center piece of bread into a small ball and tossed it into his mouth. "It's amazing," he said.

When we had all had enough to eat, Rabbi said, "Gather the leftovers so nothing is wasted."

Peter, Andrew, James, and I finished our portions and filled twelve baskets with the leftovers. As soon as the meal was finished, Rabbi instructed us to get in a boat and go across to Bethsaida while He dismissed the crowd.

CHAPTER ELEVEN

the sea

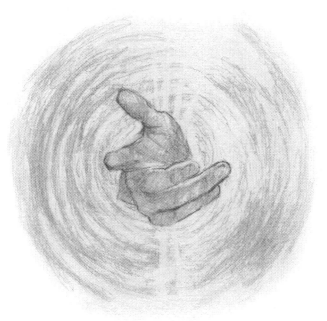

The full moon rose high above the water. Peter told the three of us to row to the other side of the lake. We sat down on the narrow plank bench at the center of the boat, propelling the group forward.

I draped my shawl across my shoulders as the wind picked up. Months away from sea had reversed my tolerance for being thrown about, and I felt the bread in my stomach rising. Burping, I settled it downward.

The non-fisherman among us were worse off. Simon and Nathanael sat clinging to the plank seat. Philip's face was pale and sweaty. Matthew held his hand over his mouth as he steadied himself over the edge.

Dark clouds settled above, and the sky moaned. I wiped my hands on my tunic. The other fisherman and I looked at each other. We knew what was brewing.

Massive droplets plopped down, soaking my hair and forcing it into my face. Moving it, I held my hand out as the trickling turned into heavy downpour.

Rabbi, where are You? It isn't safe.

Large waves crashed against the boat, filling it with water. It didn't take long for it to reach our ankles. Panicking, Thaddeus and Philip tried to plant their sandals on the slippery deck.

Judas and James the lesser grabbed their tunics and draped them over their heads and shoulders.

"What is this? What's happening?" James the lesser shouted, gripping the mast of the boat.

"What does it look like?" James said, shouting over the roar of thunder. "It's a storm! A bad one by the look of it."

"What it looks like is that we are going to die out here! All thanks to our faithful leader, Peter," Judas shouted. "Why did we go this way?"

"I've never been in the middle of a storm," Matthew yelled, shaking. He stumbled around, holding all the wrong places, and tried to get his bearings.

"Amateurs bouncing around makes me nervous, brother," James said, scooting closer to me. "Someone is bound to fall overboard."

"Not if we help them, James." I stood up. Steadying myself, I staggered toward Matthew and found him a safe place to sit.

Peter looked out of the boat. "No one is going to die. It's only a storm, and I have seen worse."

I knew he was lying. It wasn't the right season for a storm, and the clouds didn't even look like a light rain. Any fisherman could tell the signs of a storm. We wouldn't have gone out if we had known. This one seemed to spring from nowhere.

"Everyone, stay calm." Peter adjusted the sail. "Start rowing against the headwind!"

"The boat is going to flip if we don't do something. We need to get out of the water," Andrew hollered to James and me.

"It's too late," James shouted.

"What's too late?" Thomas asked. "I knew it. This storm is horrible! Judas is right. We're going to drown."

Where's Rabbi?

A wave soared beyond the height of the sail. We watched it wide-eyed like lambs waiting to be slaughtered. It crashed downward, ramming the twelve into the rim of the boat.

I sat up on my hands, but I couldn't see past the massive droplets slapping my face. "Peter, what do we do? This doesn't look like it's going to get better," I shouted.

"Is everyone still here?" he bellowed.

"Here," Andrew answered, trying to get on all fours.

Thomas grabbed his hat floating on the water inside the boat. "Here!" he whimpered.

"Here!" Simon said.

"Thaddeus and I are here," James the lesser answered, hoisting his brother up.

"Still here." Judas scowled, looking around.

"Alive, and here," James said.

"Philip? Simon? Thomas?" Peter said, searching the dark boat.

"Here!" They answered in unison, coming forward.

"We can't see to row out of this. We're going to have to wait it out," Peter said, gripping the mast.

I could see the panic on his face as he moved frantically through the boat. He didn't comment on us not rowing anymore. The water surrounded my calf. The boat wasn't going to hold much more before it went under.

Where is He?

Another wave smashed into the side of the boat, emptying the water and throwing the twelve of us back to the floor.

"We're going to die! Rabbi has abandoned us!" Judas wailed.

"Why did He take us this far to let us die?" Thomas yelled, trying to stand up.

James moved toward me. "Are you hurt?"

"No."

"What do we do, John? Maybe He's not coming back."

"Nothing is too much for Him. You know that, James."

We stood up, face-to-face, but I wasn't so sure.

"Look!" Simon shouted.

Something approached the boat, and then I remembered my dream. The dark figure that drifted across the water. It was real and moving closer.

"A ghost!" James the lesser blurted, falling backward into Judas's arms behind him.

Judas shoved James the lesser back to his feet. "It isn't real!" he shouted.

The dark figure stood calmly over the surface, moving closer and closer.

It can't be the end.

"We're dreaming!" Thomas doubted.

"How can we all imagine the same thing?" Nathanael said. "We're dead, and it's come to collect our spirits." He fell to the ground, praying as water continued to fill the boat.

"Courage! It's Me. Don't be afraid."

A bolt of lightning broke through the clouds, lighting the sea.

"Rabbi!" I shouted.

Everyone ran to the edge of the boat, staring at Rabbi.

He stood calmly in the midst of the raging storm. His tunic

tossed about His bare feet as the waves ensued around but not under His steps.

"Don't trust it! It's a ghost sent to kill us all!" Judas shouted. "It's impossible!" He ran to the back of the boat, looking for a way out.

Peter, suddenly bold, said, "Master, if it's really You, call me to come to You on the water."

"He said, 'Come ahead'."

Peter placed both hands on the edge of the boat and hoisted himself to sit on it. He slowly placed one foot onto the water. Every sense of mine waited.

Solid ground.

He placed his other foot outside the boat and began walking to Rabbi.

Wind pushed the boat farther away, and Peter stretched out both arms at his sides. Water rushed violently around him, but Rabbi stood firm with His hand out. "I can't!" Peter shouted.

The water beneath Peter's feet opened like a trap door, and he plummeted below. He tried to fight, splashing all about, but the current pulled him under. All I could see in the dark water was his arms trying to reach the surface. More waves forced his head back under.

Andrew leaned over the edge of the boat. "Peter!" he shrieked.

Peter swam to the surface, harvesting a single breath. "Master, save me!"

Rabbi went to Him. Bending over the water's surface, He reached His arm in as it gave way inches from where he stood and wrapped His hand around Peter's forearm.

Peter came to the surface gasping for air, still fighting the tight connection.

Calm down—or you'll drown.

He thrashed about, too panicked for anyone to save him. I had never seen such bewilderment. He wailed in a shrill voice, and then his body went limp. He collapsed underneath, letting go of control.

Rabbi hoisted him upward, setting him on a firm foundation

of solid water again. Rabbi wrapped His arm around Peter's waist, and he coughed up seawater, coming to. Rabbi looked at him. "Faint heart, what got into you?" They came back and got inside the boat.

The wind calmed. The storm was gone, and we were on the other side of the lake, ashore and safe. I looked at the dry ground beneath—the exact spot we were headed to.

Peter looked around silently, downcast at the boat's surface. "Rabbi, You saved me. Thank you." He looked up at Rabbi and knelt before Him. "This is it! You are God's Son for sure!"

It was clear. The acts of selflessness, kindness, healings, and exorcisms—all of it had been done by others before His time, but this night, He walked on the raging sea and silenced a storm, a miracle like no other.

The rest of us echoed, "This is it! You are God's Son for sure!"

There on the western shore in the "garden of a prince," known as Gennesaret, Rabbi and the twelve of us climbed off the boat, cold and wet.

Thomas began sorting through his things, and James the lesser knelt on the ground and kissed the soil.

Peter had us build a small fire so we could warm up.

Andrew and I gathered bits of wood. Striking two stones over our collection, we looked at each other, taken aback by His power.

A fisherman ran right through the middle of our branches. "Jesus of Nazareth!" he cried.

Soon more boats came in. "But how did He get here?" another man asked. "We searched all through Capernaum after we feasted on the loaves and fish."

"We were going to make Him our King after such a sign, but he disappeared into the mountains," the first confessed.

"We looked all night, but now He is across the lake?" one said, scratching his head.

One of Abba's hired men, Barak, came forward. He was soaked and windswept, but he always looked that way. "Rabbi, when did You get here? I watched the twelve board Peter's boat alone, but now You appear with them?"

Rabbi wrung out His tunic at the hem. "You've come looking for Me not because you saw God in My actions but because I fed you, filled your stomachs—and for free. Don't waste your energy striving for perishable food like that. Work for the food that sticks with you, food that nourishes your lasting life, food the Son of Man provides. He and what He does are guaranteed by God the Father to last."

To that, they said, "Well, what do we do then to get in on God's works?"

Why can't they see He's so much more than the miracles?

Rabbi answered, "Throw your lot in with the One who God has sent. That kind of a commitment gets you in on God's works."

Barak gave a slight frown. "Why don't You give us a clue about who You are, just a hint of what's going on? When we see what's up, we'll commit ourselves. Show us what You can do. Moses fed our ancestors with bread in the desert. It says so in the scriptures: 'He gave them bread from heaven to eat'."

"The real significance of that scripture is not that Moses gave you bread from heaven but that My Father is right now offering you bread from heaven, the real bread. The Bread of God came down out of heaven and is giving life to the world."

They jumped at that: "Master, give us this bread, now and forever!"

"I am the Bread of Life. The person who aligns with Me hungers no more and thirsts no more, ever. I have told you this explicitly because even though you have seen Me in action, you don't really believe Me. Every person the Father gives Me eventually comes running to Me. And once that person is with Me, I hold on and don't let go. I came down from heaven not to follow My own whim but to accomplish the will of the One who sent Me."

I watched the crowd shift from broad smiles to icy stares. They began to grumble and argue. "Isn't this the son of Joseph? Don't we know His father? Don't we know His mother? How can He now say, 'I came down out of heaven' and expect anyone to believe Him?"

"Don't bicker among yourselves over Me. You're not in charge here. The Father who sent Me is in charge. He draws people to Me—that's the only way you'll ever come. Only then do I do my work, putting people together, setting them on their feet, ready for the end. This is what the prophets meant when they wrote, 'And then they will all be personally taught by God.' Anyone who has spent any time at all listening to the Father, really listening and therefore learning, comes to Me to be taught personally—to see it with his own eyes, hear it with his own ears, from Me, since I have it firsthand from the Father. No one has seen the Father except the One who has His Being alongside the Father—and you can see Me.

"I'm telling you the most solemn and sober truth now: Whoever believes in Me has real life, eternal life. I am the Bread of Life. Your ancestors ate the manna bread in the desert and died, but now here is Bread that truly comes down out of heaven. Anyone eating this Bread will not die, ever. I am the Bread—living Bread!—who came down out of heaven. Anyone who eats this Bread will live—and forever! The Bread that I present to the world so that it can eat and live is Myself, this flesh-and-blood self."

Barak shouted, "How can this man serve up His flesh for a meal?"

"Only insofar as you eat and drink flesh and blood, the flesh and blood of the Son of Man, do you have life within you. The one who brings a hearty appetite to this eating and drinking has eternal life and will be fit and ready for the Final Day. My flesh is real food, and My blood is real drink. By eating My flesh and drinking My blood, you enter into Me and I into you. In the same way that the fully alive Father sent Me here and I live because of Him, so the one who makes a meal of Me lives because of Me. This is the Bread from heaven. Your ancestors ate bread and later died. Whoever eats this Bread will live always."

I felt a rush of heat over my body. It was the first time I had heard Him speak plainly to a crowd, and it was not well received. Many were upset.

Rabbi doesn't mean literally eat His flesh, but accept Him, accept the truth of His love. So that through Him you can relate to God.

An old man inched forward through the crowd. "This is tough teaching, too tough to swallow."

"Does this throw you completely? What would happen if you saw the Son of Man ascending to where He came from? The Spirit can make life. Sheer muscle and willpower don't make anything happen. Every word I've spoken to you is a Spirit-word, and so it is life-making, but some of you are resisting, refusing to have any part in this. This is why I told you earlier that no one is capable of coming to Me on his own. You get to Me only as a gift from the Father."

The old man spat on the ground, turned, and began leaving— and others followed. Many deserted Him.

Rabbi smiled and looked at us. We stood there, waiting for Him to speak. Then He asked, "Do you also want to leave?"

Peter replied, "Master, to whom would we go? You have the words of real life, eternal life. We've already committed ourselves, confident that You are the Holy One of God."

"Haven't I handpicked you, the twelve? Still, one of you is a devil!"

Devil?

CHAPTER TWELVE

the transfiguration

Almost two years since I jumped from Abba's boat to follow Rabbi, He was still dedicated, using every opportunity to teach us about the kingdom of God—unwavering in His faith and mission. However, I was constantly distracted by my dreams of foretold death and misery or by my worrisome thoughts. I couldn't shake His comment from earlier that one of us was a devil—until I discovered the traitor.

Is it me? Are my dreams a clue to my betrayal? Perhaps the darkness I saw will consume me, and I will be the one … but I would never betray Him, forsake Him—yet He was never wrong and more real than my dreams.

I didn't want to tell the others of my plan to snuff out the traitor; after all, it could be any of them. As we traveled along, I noticed the Pharisees and Sadducees waiting on the road to the synagogue. Standing there like crazed beggars, Zedekiah and Shet grabbed people as we walked by, seeking anyone who would listen to them speak against Rabbi.

"If this Rabbi is a miracle worker, let Him demonstrate so now," Zedekiah spat.

Shet hoisted himself on his toes and shouted, "Give us some hard evidence that God is in this. How about a miracle?"

He said, "You have a saying that goes, 'Red sky at night, sailor's delight; red sky at morning, sailors take warning.' You find it easy enough to forecast the weather—why can't you read the signs of the times? An evil and wanton generation is always wanting signs and wonders. The only sign you'll get is the Jonah sign." He turned on His heel and walked away.

They stood there grim-faced. Rabbi had snatched their rebuttals right out of their mouths. I hurried behind Him, needing to hear every whisper that went His way. Peter walked along at His side. "Why did they give up so easily?" I whispered.

"What can they do?"

I looked behind me and met Zedekiah's stony stare and puffed chest. "Don't you see, Peter? Rabbi's words make them angry, more often than before, and they're following us everywhere."

He looked back and shrugged. "They've done nothing but talk. It's all they ever do," he whispered.

"No, I've seen this before. Soon, insulting Him won't be enough."

Staring at Rabbi, the Baptizer's bloody head filled my mind. All I could hear were the hushed giggles of the queen and her daughter.

"John? John—"

If I had listened to the warnings. If I had trusted my dream.

"John!" Peter called.

Rabbi looked at me.

My lip quivered, and I tried to smile. "Yes, Peter," I answered, trying to sound normal.

Rabbi jostled my hair and smiled, walking on.

"See, if Rabbi is unbothered by the leader's talk, so should we."

I sighed. "If you say so."

After, He taught in the synagogue and led us out of Bethsaida—to the pagan city Caesarea, Philippi, north of the sea.

Caesarea, Philippi, the gate of Hades—they called it. My eyes were glued to carvings of false gods etched into the foot of Mount Hermon. Standing at the crux of it, I tilted my head and took in the shrine of stone faces and body parts in mingled positions. We were forbidden as a people from going anywhere near the city, yet here we were, staring—no ogling—the mountain—all except Rabbi and Peter. The rest of the twelve came up behind me, wide-eyed and beaming.

Simon snickered and nudged me forward. "Look, over there. It's Pan. A man with the legs of a goat. The Greek god of fertility. How does one become a goat-man? Does a girl marry a goat … or give birth—"

"It's not funny. An entire city of lost people. We should pity them," Philip said, looking down at the dirt road.

"Why pity them?" Simon asked, still staring.

"Don't look," Philip said. "They believe this is the gate to the underworld and worshipping these things will surely summon something."

"Interesting. Seems their gods give complete freedom. They can do whatever they please," Simon continued.

Thaddaeus walked over. For the silent type, you could still see what he was thinking. He cocked his head with a long groan. "It's wrong to cater to one's every desire," he said, looking at the mountain.

Judas clutched the money bag, shifting back and forth. "Worshipping a bunch of rocks? Crazy," he added with an enormous swallow. "I can't imagine holding a rock in my hand and expecting it to answer my prayers."

"Technically, you can see a rock. Whereas the evidence for our God is harder to see," James the lesser interjected.

"Our God made the world in seven days," said James.

"I know our God is great," James the lesser agreed. "I can't imagine bowing to a carving I made with my own hands, hoping it'll give my wife children or bring me wealth. It's craziness. Like Judas said."

I didn't have anything to add. The ordinary Greek or Roman would never concern themselves with us, outside the taxes they collected. My attention was on Rabbi and Peter. *What were they talking about? The devil among us?*

Rabbi cleared His throat, standing underneath the sordid symbols. The others stopped muttering. He stroked His beard and turned to us. "What are people saying about who the Son of Man is?"

Nathanael offered, "Some think He is John the Baptizer."

The Baptizer? Had he been the Son of Man, he would be alive. God would have protected His Son.

Thomas took off his hat and scratched his head. "Some say Elijah, some—"

"Wrong." Judas interrupted. "Jeremiah or one of the other prophets."

"And how about you? Who do you say I am?"

Peter said, "You're the Christ, the Messiah, the Son of the living God."

Everyone was quiet. It seemed that most of the twelve had accepted Rabbi as a prophet, a miracle worker, but they hadn't considered Him the Son of God.

"God bless you, Simon, son of Jonah! You didn't get that answer out of books or from teachers. My Father in heaven, God himself, let you in on this secret of who I really am. And now I'm going to tell you who you *really* are. You are Peter, a rock. This is the rock on which I will put together my church, a church so expansive with energy that not even the gates of hell will be able to keep it out." He pointed to the mountain.

Drawing closer to the mountain, I tried to see what He did. In pagan cities like this one—of the broken and the lost—Rabbi would build His church. Then, He swore us to secrecy, making us promise not to tell anyone what He had said.

I was happy to keep it to myself. Beheading wouldn't be enough if the leaders heard Him say He was the Son of God. He said, "It is necessary that the Son of Man proceed to an ordeal of suffering, be tried and found guilty by the religious leaders, high priests, and religion scholars, be killed, and on the third day be raised up alive."

What?

Peter took Him in hand, saying, "Impossible, Master! That can never be!"

Killed? Found guilty? My heart sank as I fell into the dungeon of my thoughts. *I won't let them! I'll kill every one of them if I have to. I'm not going to stand by and do nothing—not again. They're never going to hurt anyone, ever ... God wouldn't let harm come to His Son? I know what to do.*

He penetrated my inner dialogue to add, "Anyone who intends to come with Me has to let Me lead. You're not in the driver's seat—I am. Don't run from suffering; embrace it. Follow Me. I'll show you how. Self-help is no help at all. Self-sacrifice is the way, My way, to finding yourself, your true self. What good would it do to get everything you want and lose you, the real you? If any of you is embarrassed with Me and the way I'm leading you, know that the

Son of Man will be far more embarrassed with you when He arrives in all His splendor in company with the Father and the holy angels. This isn't, you realize, pie in the sky by and by. Some who have taken their stand right here are going to see it happen, see with their own eyes the kingdom of God."

The twelve of us wore confused faces, but we didn't question Him. My mind began to carefully construct His death and what would happen to me if I tried to stop the leaders. *Dead at fourteen. What if they come tonight?*

I ran my hand through my hair, thinking about all the missed opportunities. I closed my eyes, leaned my head back, dragged the tension in my neck into my shoulders, and thought of seemingly simpler times. *The Jordan, cool water. Standing there with nothing to do but wait. Until the day the Baptizer spoke of the Messiah.*

I opened my eyes, realizing I now stood in the midst of that truth.

Andrew elbowed me. "What does it all mean, John?" he whispered.

"It's like the Baptizer," I said. "It didn't make sense—until now. We never knew he was right about the Messiah, but here we are."

Andrew rubbed his head. "That's true. If only we knew then what we do now. And what's next?"

I sighed. "I don't know."

Six days later, Rabbi took Peter, James, and me up a high mountain. I hadn't considered before then the regularity for which He called us away, but as we hiked away, I could see resistance from the others. I know it was tempting for them to wonder why us, but we were among the first He called.

The one whom He loved, but I'm not worthy. I was grateful to be chosen and hoped I would have the chance to ask about His prophecy. We gathered around Him, kneeling with both palms pressed together—fingertips to the sky—as He led us in prayer. I was angry at the thought of losing Him, but I didn't want to miss a moment of quiet time with Him.

A short silence was attacked by searing light through my eyelids. I opened them, wincing at the brightness, and His face was like the sun. His clothes shimmered, glistening white, whiter than any bleach could make them.

God is taking Him, protecting Him from the leaders.

Shaking, I looked over to James and Peter. They were perfectly still. I shielded my face with my arm. Looking around, two men were standing with Him.

My mouth opened when I heard their names: Moses and Elijah. I knelt inches from the author of the teachings. *The* Moses. Known for using his staff, with the power of God, to part the Red Sea—freeing our people from slavery in Egypt—hundreds of years before.

But he's dead. Has been for centuries. Though no one knew where he was buried. Now he's standing here talking to Rabbi—who is completely unbothered by his deadness. Though he looks normal, alive, not dead.

A faint whisper in my ear, "Is that Elijah?" James asked. "Prophet? Bringer of fire from heaven?"

I inhaled, putting both hands on my head. "It is."

And there we were, waiting while Rabbi and two deceased Israelite heroes talked like casual friends. Then I heard it. I wanted them to be there for no reason—a chance meeting of sorts. Instead, they spoke of His departure, which He was about to bring to fulfillment in Jerusalem.

Peter said, "Rabbi, this is a great moment! Let's build three memorials—one for you, one for Moses, one for Elijah."

While he was babbling, a light-radiant cloud enveloped them, and from deep in the cloud, a voice said, "This is My Son, marked by My love. Listen to Him."

We fell facedown to the ground, terrified.

God? This is it. Rabbi's leaving.

But then Rabbi came and touched me on the shoulder. "Don't be afraid."

When I looked up, there was no one except Him. I sighed, relieved.

Rabbi smiled and led us back down the mountain to the rest of the twelve. As we were coming down the mountain, He instructed, "Don't breathe a word of what you've seen. After the Son of Man is raised from the dead, you are free to talk."

"What does He mean risen from the dead?" I whispered to James.

"I don't know, but if we ever had doubts about Rabbi, they've been answered today." James looked behind him. "Where did they go?"

Peter looked at Rabbi. "Everything is as predicted in the scrolls, except why do the religion scholars say that Elijah has to come first?"

"Elijah does come and get everything ready. I'm telling you, Elijah has already come, but they didn't know him when they saw him.

The Baptizer. He was the Elijah the scrolls referred to. He prepared the way.

Rabbi added, "They treated him like dirt—the same way they are about to treat the Son of Man."

No, they are not.

When we got back to town, we walked along the road and saw a crowd gathering. We tried to make our way through.

Someone yelled, "Liars!"

I saw Judas and Bartholomew arguing with the leaders.

"Even though we cannot do what He does, He is still a good Rabbi. He obeys the law. *You're* wrong," Bartholomew said to Zedekiah.

"Where is He?" Zedekiah barked back. "If you do not leave this heretic, who ignores our beliefs and traditions, you will be expelled from the temple!"

"Only the high priest and the Sanhedrin have that power," Judas said. "All matters concerning the people must be decided by the *entire* Sanhedrin."

Shet sneered at Judas. "You know nothing, boy! You would rather continue to be led astray by a conspirator than understand. He is a demon-possessed liar! We do not need to dissuade you and the rest of the twelve from continuing at His side. You will be dealt with by the high priest."

Philip threw up his hands. "I have had enough of the arguing. You seek to bully and intimidate us, but what do the teachings say of oppressing others?"

Shet said, "You are not being oppressed! You are being duly warned!"

Simon scowled. "I have heard about you! You aren't worried about who we follow. You only want political growth within the synagogue, dear Sadducee."

We reached them. Many ran up to greet Rabbi. Andrew was the only one silent. Shet walked up to him and said, "What will you do? Each of you has a choice." He stared at Rabbi and pointed. "Will you follow this fabricator to His demise?"

Andrew sighed. "Teacher, do you seek to isolate our Rabbi by turning us against Him? You want Him to suffer for speaking against you and the others, but we will not leave Him."

Zedekiah shook his head. "No, I see the worry in your faces. You are but young men, too young to be killed. Will you die for Him? How many of you have lived long enough to taste death? Will you throw everything away for a mere man?"

I've had enough. "We will never leave Him! You are wasting your time! Surely men of your importance have bigger matters than the minds of wayward boys!"

Rabbi gave me a look, and I knew I needed to be quiet. He asked, "What's going on? What's all the commotion?"

A man out of the crowd answered, "Teacher, I brought my mute son, made speechless by a demon, to You. Whenever it seizes him, it throws him to the ground. He foams at the mouth, grinds his teeth, and goes stiff as a board." He gripped his son's hand firmly. The boy's bloody knees showed through his shapeless tunic. "They could not deliver him."

"Rabbi, we tried everything," Simon confessed.

The boy flashed a cruel grin at me as I stared. Whatever inhabited him knew it had my full attention. He mimed words to me: "In the spirit." Struggling to loosen his father's grip, he taunted me.

"They're unable to help because they lack demonic possession like their so-called Rabbi. It is from evil means from which He draws His power," Zedekiah said.

"What a generation! No sense of God! How many times do I have to go over these things? How much longer do I have to put up with this? Bring the boy here." He held His hand out to the father.

But the demon within didn't want to come near Rabbi. It threw the boy to the ground where he jerked about, rolling and contorting and foaming at the mouth.

He asked the boy's father, "How long has this been going on?"

"Ever since he was a little boy. Many times, it pitches him into fire or the river to do away with him. If you can do anything, do it. Have a heart and help us!"

"If? There are no 'ifs' among believers. Anything can happen."

No sooner were the words out of his mouth than the father cried, "Then I believe. Help me with my doubts!"

"Dumb and deaf spirit, I command you! Out of him—and stay out!"

Screaming, and with much thrashing about, it left. The boy was pale as a corpse, and people started saying, "He's dead."

Rabbi knelt down, took his hand, and helped him up.

The crowd cheered.

The man ran to his son, embracing him and weeping joyously.

I never thought to ask for help in my belief, but somehow the stranger knew. To heal, to perform miracles, to overcome the leaders, I needed Him. "Rabbi, help me overcome my unbelief," I whispered to myself.

Simon came to Rabbi's side. "Why couldn't we throw the demon out?"

He answered, "There is no way to get rid of this kind of demon except by prayer."

After it happened, we left that place and passed through Galilee. Rabbi made it clear He didn't want anyone to know where we were because He needed the opportunity to teach us further. Things were rushed, off somehow. Our time together was limited.

One night, He brought us close. "The Son of Man is about to be betrayed to some people who want nothing to do with God. They will murder Him. Three days after His murder, He will rise, alive."

I didn't understand why it had to happen, why He kept saying such an awful thing, but I was afraid to ask. It was the second time He spoke of His death. I felt empty. I didn't want to hear another word of it until I was ready with a plan.

CHAPTER THIRTEEN

pharisees

Autumn brought an eight-day celebration, the Festival of Tabernacles. Tradition commanded we join thousands journeying with home tied to their backs and those they loved—to the center of our faith—where Rabbi prophesied He would be murdered: Jerusalem. Symphonies of flutist carried through the air, thanking God, asking Him to provide crops for the coming year.

Familiar sounds sparked memories of when James and I had taken the same route with Abba and mother. Oh, how we used to swap blows behind the family cart to her horror! I grinned, recalling that she would wrap her hand around mine, separating us. She always gripped a little firmer, crouching down to whisper in my ear, "Remember, son, the festival marks crueler times. Our people spent generations enslaved by the Egyptians until Moses set us free. We celebrate the most essential necessity: water. Even now, its scarcity requires continual reliance on God. It's in our dependence that we truly understand His glory."

Sharing stories of our people was a long-practiced custom. I paid such little attention then, but as I thought about her words, I realized their importance looking at Rabbi.

He stopped ahead, and turned to us, "Listen to Me carefully." He looked us in the eyes like He was ready for what was coming. "We're on our way up to Jerusalem. When we get there, the Son of Man will be betrayed to the religious leaders and scholars. They will sentence Him to death. Then they will hand Him over to the Romans, who will mock and spit on Him, give Him the third degree, and kill Him. After three days, He will rise alive."

Not again.

Warmth rushed over me. My throat tightened, and I felt nauseous. His third warning was hard enough without becoming more detailed—and now here we stood.

Why did He bring us? Does He want to die?

Peter was glaring at the ground. "Is there nothing we can do?" I whispered.

"When the time is right, we will act. I bought something in the last town. It will help us. *If* we need it," he answered.

"Bought something?"

"I will handle it. You're too young. I know what to do," he said, but his relaxed demeanor made me think otherwise. "Let's go to the festival and be on our guard. For now, that's all we can do."

I wanted to try my chances with James or the rest of the twelve, but their silence made me distrust them. None of them understood Rabbi's prediction. I had the displeasure of shadowed dreams that happened too often to downplay it all. I couldn't risk indecision or secret plans. The Baptizer's powerlessness to save himself should have been a blistered keepsake to us, but it seemed that I alone refused to let Rabbi suffer the same fate. I stayed close as we climbed the steps to the wolves' lair.

Behind me, a familiar voice said, "John, James!"

"Mother?" I said, turning around. It was an odd coincidence since I was just thinking about her.

"My sons," she shouted and made her way through the crowd.

James heard and came to us. "Mother."

I smiled as she embraced me and then James. I wanted to share everything of my journey and all that had happened, but I couldn't shake the importance of Rabbi entering the temple without me.

Rabbi and the others stopped ahead near the entrance as the crowd separated us.

"How are things?" James asked her.

My troubled mind could no more care for their conversation than I could fly over the people to Rabbi. I refused to make the same mistake I had made with the Baptizer. "We have to go," I interrupted, avoiding her wanting eyes.

"I am happy to see you. You are men ... grown so much." She caressed my cheek, tracing my jawline as I looked around her head to Rabbi coming our way. She lingered. "We need not discuss things now; our time will come."

"Shalom," the others greeted her.

She didn't respond, staring open-mouthed at Rabbi. All at once, she knelt before Him. "May I ask You a favor?" She reached for His hand at His side.

"What is it you want?"

She said, "Give Your word that these two sons of mine will be awarded the highest places of honor in Your kingdom, one at Your right hand, one at Your left hand."

"You have no idea what you're asking." He turned to us and said, "Are you capable of drinking the cup that I'm about to drink?"

"Sure, why not?" James and I answered. Looking back on it, I said the words before I understood what it meant.

"Come to think of it, you are going to drink My cup, but as to awarding places of honor, that's not My business. My Father is taking care of that."

I looked at the others. Peter eyed James and me like we were sheep feces. Judas muttered to himself with arms crossed. I tried to make out the words, but it was probably for the best I couldn't hear. The others ate her bitter words, and it presented on their faces. I understood why they were so thoroughly disgusted. None of them had seen their families in a long time, and now my mother was asking for a position above them. I always felt like my mother wanted me to do big things—bigger than I wanted for myself. Thinking on it longer, I was mortified by her promotion and what she had requested.

Rabbi turned and headed for the temple. "Goodbye, Mother," we said in unison and followed Him. She disappeared into the crowd. Even though I knew she had made her request in an effort to help us, as the others passed by James and me, indignant, I didn't know how I was going to make things right.

Simon shoved me as he walked by. "Sure, why not?" he mocked.

"Fools," Thomas whispered to my left.

Judas turned his head and leered at us. "Who do you two think you are?" he whispered.

More shoves, until we were at the back of the group.

Rabbi called us together at the threshold of the temple, resting his arms on Simon and Peter. We huddled together, and He said, "You've observed how godless rulers throw their weight around, how quickly a little power goes to their heads. It's not going to be that way with you. Whoever wants to be great must become a servant. Whoever wants to be first among you must be your slave. That is what the Son of Man has done. He came to serve, not be served—and then to give away His life in exchange for the many who are held hostage."

The true leader among us would give up everything, refusing to gain anything for himself. At the moment, I didn't think any of us were ready to do that.

Thousands waited to fill the room. Those inside parted, making way for the leaders. Zedekiah strutted in alongside the most powerful among them, the high priest. Joseph Caiaphas was the only person who could convene the Sanhedrin—seventy-one members of men—deciding the fate of civil and religious teachings, judge of us all.

Gossip told the story that his role came from his wife's father, who previously held the position and that he spent his life trying to prove suitable—though he had no real expertise. He didn't talk much, but when he did, everyone listened. After spending time with the Baptizer and Rabbi, it was clear the little he did say came from a desire to preserve the teachings and not to live by them.

I gritted my teeth at His expensive tunic and jeweled headpiece when He stopped in front of us and turned his back. He squinted an eye at Rabbi, bending bushy gray eyebrows. He didn't say anything to Him; he just whispered behind his gray beard to Zedekiah.

This was my moment. I could reach out and tug his robe and refute all the negative things he had heard about Rabbi and convince him Rabbi was love and kindness, undeserving of his rage. I planned all the things I could say, but nothing came out of my mouth. All I could recall was Abba's instruction to avoid any discussions of any kind when in his presence, to show him the reverence of the "most important being." For a long time, I had thought he was deserving of such importance, but not now. Only Rabbi was worthy of that title. Still, I couldn't make myself let go of what I was taught to do, for what I needed to.

"Look," a little girl said, pointing. "It's Jesus, the Son of God." She tugged on her father's clothes.

"Be silent child—or they will hear you," her father instructed.

The others realized Rabbi was behind the high priest and began giving their opinions. Some said, "He's a good man." Others said, "Not so. He's selling snake oil."

I understood why they were afraid to acknowledge Him. I could sense it in the pit of my stomach—the conflict—the chance to be set apart and the desire to fit in. The leaders in Jerusalem were the center of our faith and were far more brutal to any disruptions in tradition than local leaders.

A bead of sweat tickled my cheek, and I beheld the most dangerous place in the world for a Man who claimed to be the Son of God. I took in every stone column, every bit of cobbled floor, and watched for hidden attackers. "We may have to fight," I whispered to James.

James stood behind me. "You're right, but we can't save everyone. I'm ready to protect you in case anything happens."

Me? What about the others? What about Rabbi?

"Did you hear me?" James asked.

My eyes were fixed on Caiaphas. Rabbi didn't bother with formalities and moved in front, standing on the bema. "A man planted a vineyard. He fenced it, dug a winepress, erected a watchtower, turned it over to the farmhands, and went off on a trip. At the time for harvest, he sent a servant back to the farmhands to collect his profits.

"They grabbed him, beat him up, and sent him off empty-handed. So he sent another servant. That one, they tarred and feathered. He sent another, and that one they killed. And on and on, many others. Some they beat up, and some they killed.

"Finally, there was only one left: a beloved son. In a last-ditch effort, he sent him, thinking, *Surely, they will respect my son.*

"But those farmhands saw their chance. They rubbed their hands together in greed and said, 'This is the heir! Let's kill him and have it all for ourselves.' They grabbed him, killed him, and threw him over the fence.

"What do you think the owner of the vineyard will do? Right. He'll come and clean house. Then he'll assign the care of the vineyard to others. Read it for yourselves in scripture:

That stone the masons threw out
is now the cornerstone!
This is God's work;
we rub our eyes—we can hardly believe it!

James leaned over, "Why does He speak in parables? What does it mean?"

"Remember when Rabbi said, 'You've been given insight into God's kingdom—you know how it works, but to those who can't see it yet, everything comes in stories, creating readiness, nudging them toward receptive insight. These are people—

Whose eyes are open but don't see a thing,
Whose ears are open but don't understand a word,
Who avoid making an about-face and getting forgiven.

"How did you remember that verbatim?" James asked. "You didn't answer my question, smart one."

"In the parable, the owner of the vineyard is God, and the tenants are the leaders of the temple. The ones sent are the prophets from the past. According to our history, the prophets have been beaten and mistreated by the leaders. The owner decides to send His own son, believing they will treat the one he loves with kindness. Instead, they hate him the most and kill him. Rab—"

"Rabbi is the Son, sent by the owner," James interrupted.

"Exactly," I answered with a sigh.

"What do we do?" James asked.

"Wait and hope we can stop it—this time," I said, looking at Him.

"This time?"

"Never mind." I wasn't interested in clarifying. Someone across from us was exceptionally red-faced and bore a hole into Rabbi's forehead. I struggled to recognize him among the Pharisees. "Who is that, James?"

"I don't know, but here he comes."

"He's so angry. Get ready in case he starts something."

"Sit down, Saul!" Zedekiah instructed, pulling at his arm.

"No! Listen to Him," Saul said. "Hear His words. He openly suggests the prophecies are answered through Him."

I read Zedekiah's tightened lips: "I know, but we must wait for the right opportunity."

"For what, more blasphemies?" Saul said. "The audacity! There has been no confirmation by the authorities of the law that Jesus is to be trusted as authentic, yet so many support Him."

"I do not support Him!" Zedekiah blurted, standing up.

The room stirred, looking at the two men.

Zedekiah gave a fake grin. "The high priest will speak. We must wait," he said in a hushed voice.

"I know nothing of that plan. It's cowardice to sit here waiting." Saul walked closer, pushing toward Rabbi. "How does He know so much without being schooled?"

"I didn't make this up. What I teach comes from the One who sent Me. Anyone who wants to do His will can test this teaching and know whether it's from God or whether I'm making it up. A person making things up tries to make himself look good, but someone trying to honor the One who sent him sticks to the facts and doesn't tamper with reality. It was Moses, wasn't it, who gave you God's Law? But none of you are living it. So why are you trying to kill Me?"

"You're crazy! Who's trying to kill you? You're demon-possessed."

"I did one miraculous thing a few months ago, and you're still standing around getting all upset, wondering what I'm up to. Moses prescribed circumcision—originally it came not from Moses but from his ancestors—and so you circumcise a man, dealing with one part of his body, even if it's the Sabbath. You do this in order to preserve one item in the Law of Moses. So why are you upset with Me because I made a man's whole body well on the Sabbath? Don't be nitpickers. Use your heads—and hearts! —to discern what is right, to test what is authentically right."

Saul spun in a circle. Stiff, he snapped, "Isn't this the One they were out to kill? And here He is out in the open, saying whatever He pleases, and no one is stopping Him. Could it be that the rulers know that He is, in fact, the Messiah? And yet we know where this Man came from. The Messiah is going to come out of nowhere. Nobody is going to know where he comes from."

"Yes, you think you know Me and where I'm from, but that's not where I'm from. I didn't set Myself up in business. My true origin is in the One who sent Me, and you don't know Him at all. I come from Him—that's how I know Him. He sent Me here."

Someone among the people stood. "Will the Messiah, when He comes, provide better or more convincing evidence than this?"

The Pharisees, alarmed at this seditious undertow going through the crowd, teamed up with the high priests and sent their police to arrest Him. "Come get him, down from here! It is enough!" Caiaphas demanded, colliding the bottom of his cane with the floor.

Caiaphas's guards appeared from behind pillars and nooks within the temple, like mice scurrying toward a single morsel. They lunged toward Him, pushing all of us to the ground.

Zedekiah crept from the bench, staring at Rabbi with half-lidded eyes. My eyes focused on his mocking smile as he came closer. Reaching past me, he tripped just short of Rabbi over my legs and fell on top of me. "You!" he shouted with the sour breath of a corpse.

I squirmed, trying to get him off me, but I was afraid to hurt him. His limbs trembled over mine like weathered tree branches. He clamored to his knees as they sounded on the cobbled floor.

The chaos of the leaders pushing and shoving through the crowd made it impossible for us to stand. I could only watch as they tried to seize Him. Searching for others in the brawl, I saw my chance and rolled Zedekiah to his side, staggering to my feet. I stood, holding my hand out to Him.

Zedekiah was a thousand years old and seconds from being trampled. "This changes nothing, boy," he muttered, sweating and sunken.

I hoisted him up in one motion to an unsteadied stance. Crooked, he lifted his shawl, revealing bruises and scrapes on his pale legs.

The other leaders pushed forward, though their attempts were repeated misses. The very hand of God surrounded His Son, protecting Him from a single misguided hand. "I am with you only a short time. Then I go on to the One who sent Me. You will look for Me, but you won't find Me. Where I am, you can't come."

The room grew silent.

Saul said, "Where do you think He is going that we won't be able to find Him? Do you think He is about to travel to the Greek world to teach the Jews? What is He talking about, anyway? 'You will look for Me, but you won't find Me.' 'Where I am, you can't come'?"

He cried out, "If anyone thirsts, let him come to Me and drink. Rivers of living water will brim and spill out of the depths of anyone who believes in Me this way, just as the scripture says."

In the crowd, someone shouted, "This has to be the Prophet!"

"He is the Messiah!"

Others were saying, "The Messiah doesn't come from Galilee, does He? Don't the scriptures tell us that the Messiah comes from David's line and from Bethlehem, David's village?"

His story, which He had told many times, filled my mind, but not my mouth. *Born in Bethlehem during the census of Herod. A lineage traced to King David, His parents fled the mass murder of every infant boy, to save His life. Years later, they returned home, raising Him in Nazareth.*

I balled my hands, wanting to say everything I knew, but Rabbi shook His head at me.

"I am the world's Light. No one who follows Me stumbles around in the darkness. I provide plenty of light to live in."

The Pharisees objected, saying, "All we have is Your word on this. We need more than this to go on."

"You're right that you only have My word, but you can depend on it being true. I know where I've come from and where I go next. You don't know where I'm from or where I'm headed. You decide according to what you can see and touch. I don't make judgments like that, but even if I did, My judgment would be true because I wouldn't make it out of the narrowness of my experience but in the largeness of the One who sent Me: the Father. That fulfills the conditions set down in God's Law: that you can count on the testimony of two witnesses. And that is what you have: You have My word, and you have the word of the Father who sent Me."

They said, "Where is this so-called Father of Yours?"

"You're looking right at Me, and you don't see Me. How do you expect to see the Father? If you knew Me, you would at the same time know the Father."

Zedekiah glared at Him. "This is absurd! You claim to be the guiding light of God, like that given as a beacon in the wilderness to our ancestors?"

Shet went to the front of the room, grabbed the scroll off the bema, and held it up. "Not only that, brother. He claims acceptance of such will save whoever believes. Giving Himself the power to grant believers access to God. Therefore, we do not need the teachings. According to Him, all is fulfilled."

Then He went over the same ground again, saying, "I'm leaving, and you are going to look for Me, but you're missing God in this and are headed for a dead end. There is no way you can come with Me."

Zedekiah said, "So is He going to kill himself? Is that what he means by 'You can't come with Me'?"

"You're tied down to the mundane. I'm in touch with what is

beyond your horizons. You live in terms of what you see and touch. I'm living on other terms. I told you that you were missing God in all this. You're at a dead end. If you won't believe I am who I say I am, you're at the dead end of sins. You're missing God in your lives."

Saul said, "Just who are You anyway?"

"What I've said from the start. I have so many things to say that concern you, judgments to make that affect you, but if you don't accept the trustworthiness of the One who commanded My words and acts, none of it matters. That is who you are questioning—not Me but the One who sent Me."

They still didn't get it, not realizing that He was referring to the Father.

"When you raise up the Son of Man, then you will know who I am—that I'm not making this up, but speaking only what the Father taught Me. The One who sent Me stays with Me. He doesn't abandon Me. He sees how much joy I take in pleasing Him."

"I believe!" someone shouted.

"I do!" another sounded.

A woman exclaimed, "The Messiah has come!"

"Then you will experience for yourselves the truth, and the truth will free you."

Shet, mouth opened, declared, "But we're descendants of Abraham. We've never been slaves to anyone. How can You say, 'The truth will free you'?"

"I tell you most solemnly that anyone who chooses a life of sin is trapped in a dead-end life and is, in fact, a slave. A slave is a transient, who can't come and go at will. The Son, though, has an established position, the run of the house. So, if the Son sets you free, you are free through and through. I know you are Abraham's descendants, but I also know that you are trying to kill Me because My message hasn't yet penetrated your thick skulls. I'm talking about things I have seen while keeping company with the Father, and you just go on doing what you have heard from your father."

"Our father is Abraham!"

"If you were Abraham's children, you would have been doing the things Abraham did. And yet here you are trying to kill Me, a man who has spoken to you the truth He got straight from God! Abraham never did that sort of thing. You persist in repeating the works of your father."

They said, "We're not bastards. We have a legitimate father: the one and only God."

"If God were your father," said Rabbi, "you would love Me, for I came from God and arrived here. I didn't come on My own. He sent Me. Why can't you understand one word I say? Here's why: You can't handle it. You're from your father, the devil, and all you want to do is please him. He was a killer from the very start. He couldn't stand the truth because there wasn't a shred of truth in him. When the liar speaks, he makes it up out of his lying nature and fills the world with lies. I arrive on the scene, tell you the plain truth, and you refuse to have a thing to do with Me. Can any one of you convict Me of a single misleading word, a single sinful act? But if I'm telling the truth, why don't you believe Me? Anyone on God's side listens to God's words. This is why you're not listening—because you're not on God's side."

Saul threw up his hands. "That clinches it. We were right all along when we called You a Samaritan and said You were crazy—demon-possessed!"

"I'm not crazy. I simply honor My Father while you dishonor Me. I am not trying to get anything for Myself. God intends something gloriously grand here and is making the decisions that will bring it about. I say this with absolute confidence. If you practice what I'm telling you, you'll never have to look death in the face."

Zedekiah huffed. "Now we know you're crazy. Abraham died. The prophets died. And You show up saying, 'If you practice what I'm telling you, you'll never have to face death, not even a taste.' Are you greater than Abraham, who died? And the prophets died! Who do You think You are!"

"If I turned the spotlight on Myself, it wouldn't amount to

anything, but My Father, the same One you say is your Father, put Me here at this time and place of splendor. You haven't recognized Him in this, but I have. If I, in false modesty, said I didn't know what was going on, I would be as much of a liar as you are, but I do know, and I am doing what He says. Abraham—your 'father'—with jubilant faith looked down the corridors of history and saw My day coming. He saw it and cheered."

Saul interjected, "You're not even fifty years old—and Abraham saw You?"

"Believe Me," said Rabbi, "*I am who I am* long before Abraham was anything."

That did it—pushing them over the edge—and they picked up rocks to throw at Him.

Peter shouted to us. "Come on."

We struggled through, moving to Rabbi, except one.

In the darkened corner, Judas was with Caiaphas.

CHAPTER FOURTEEN

satan

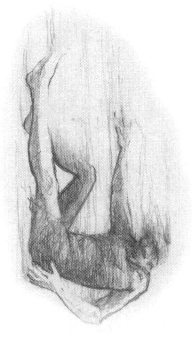

Blinding light. Standing in the center of a coliseum was a man with pure white wings of a giant falcon, dressed in snowy armor. Taller than the others, he stood majestic and powerful. Cheering, those in seats stood and celebrated. "Lucifer, son of the morning!" Hurrying toward him, they ascended down steps to the center. He smiled, taking it in, but the slight frown at the corner of his mouth meant it wasn't enough.

Seconds later, he argued with a man made of light. Lucifer grated his teeth and paced along the dense greenery of a garden. The sound of one row of molars against the other tortured the silence. His own light began to fade, turning him black. "He's wrong … a fool," he grumbled to himself. Making things worse, he refused to be cast out alone. He fled. Lying, he condemned the others in his army to follow.

"Not worthy of worship?" they asked.

Grinning, he corrupted them. Cast down, shrilling, and bellowing, he fell from heaven like lightning to earth. Dense clouds gave way to his falling body. Fire encircled him, turning his wings to dust. On the ground—disfigured—he was left to walk in the shadow of men.

Now, the enemy of good, he scoured the earth with those he stole possessing and persuading humans to error.

I stood in a black void, and Lucifer crept behind me, breathing in my ear. "I'm coming for Him. Death is not enough!" he growled. I strained to see as he pointed at Judas. Judas deflated into the surface of the black. He walked to him, stepping into his flesh like a pair of trousers. Warped and twisted, his eyes replaced Judas's. The two were now one.

I woke. Soaked, I sat up. Breath held, wanting to scream, but afraid the sound would choke me, I looked around the room. Rabbi at my side. Everyone was asleep, except one. Wicked black eyes met me, below them half-teeth seized the night. The devil within reached a hand out, beckoning me. The familiarity should have sent me running, but I could no more leave His side than snuff out the darkness in my friend. "In the spirit," it taunted in a growl. He knew me. I shook my head, refusing to go to him. His finger moved to his lips. Confronted by my dream, I knew my gift had finally explained its purpose—to stand between them—no matter what buried itself into Judas.

Sitting there staring at him made me think of the first time he came for Rabbi—the story of what happened in the desert before He called. We needed to remember every word and every detail of His teachings. We weren't learned scribes. We didn't have papyrus paper to detail what He taught—only our memories, sharpened by years reciting the teachings.

I remembered verbatim as I had been taught.

Rabbi spoke of the journey after His baptism. The missing forty days and nights. Hidden in the desert was the devil. Lead by the Spirit, Rabbi fasted, preparing for their encounter. That left him, of course, in a state of extreme hunger, which the devil took advantage of in the first test: "Since You are God's Son, speak the word that will turn these stones into loaves of bread."

Rabbi answered by quoting the teachings of Moses: "It takes more than bread to stay alive. It takes a steady stream of words from God's mouth."

For the second test, the devil took him to the Holy City, sat Him on top of the temple, and said, "Since you are God's Son, jump." The devil goaded him by quoting Psalm 91: "He has placed You in the care of angels. They will catch You so that You won't so much as stub Your toe on a stone."

He countered with another citation from Deuteronomy: "Don't you dare test the Lord your God."

Quickly, the devil took Him to the peak of a huge mountain. He gestured expansively, pointing out all the earth's kingdoms, how glorious they all were. Then he said, "They're Yours—lock, stock, and barrel. Just go down on Your knees and worship me, and they're Yours."

His refusal was curt: "Beat it, Satan!" He backed His rebuke with a third quotation from Deuteronomy: "Worship the Lord your God, and only Him. Serve Him with absolute single-heartedness."

The test was over. The devil left. And in his place, angels! Angels came and took care of Rabbi's needs.

Now, the devil—once called son of the morning—hunted Him.

The winter morning brought more darkness, and I stalked the traitor. I wasn't letting my guard down, especially on our return to Jerusalem. Following behind Rabbi and the rest of the twelve, we entered the temple courts for the Festival of Dedication. Another symbol of what Rabbi embodied in flesh, it reminded our people of the temple's restoration under Judah Maccabee, who in a fit of rebellion removed unwelcomed statues of Greek deities.

We passed along the walkway of Solomon's Colonnade, the same doors where they had tried to seize Him. I lost Judas, focusing my gaze on Zedekiah and the high priest. They rushed around us like bees, creating an impenetrable circle of old flesh and clout.

The high priest gave his instructions, clutching Zedekiah's arm. "Trap Him in His words. We must get the Sanhedrin to see what we see. There can be no doubt regarding His blasphemies."

Zedekiah glared at Rabbi. "How long are you going to keep us guessing? If you're the Messiah, tell us straight out."

Speaking the words demanded death.

"I told you, but you don't believe. Everything I have done has been authorized by My Father, actions that speak louder than words. You don't believe because you're not My sheep. My sheep recognize My voice. I know them, and they follow Me. I give them real and eternal life. They are protected from the destroyer for good. No one can steal them from out of My hand. The Father who put them under My care is so much greater than the destroyer and thief. No one could ever get them away from him. I and the Father are one heart and mind."

The twelve of us looked in horror at the leaders bending down to grasp stones beneath them. "I have made a present to you from the Father of a great many good actions. For which of these acts do you stone Me?"

Zedekiah shook a jagged rock. "We're not stoning you for anything good You did, but for what You said—this blasphemy of calling Yourself God."

"I'm only quoting your inspired scriptures, where God said, 'I tell you—you are gods.' If God called your ancestors 'gods'—and scripture doesn't lie—why do you yell, 'Blasphemer! Blasphemer!' at the unique One the Father consecrated and sent into the world, just because I said, 'I am the Son of God'? If I don't do the things My Father does, well and good; don't believe Me, but if I am doing them, put aside for a moment what you hear Me say about Myself and just take the evidence of the actions that are right before your eyes. Then perhaps things will come together for you, and you'll see that not only are we doing the same thing, we are the same—Father and Son. He is in Me; I am in Him."

The circle opened, and the guards moved in. I ran to His side, but the rest of the twelve hid. I still couldn't find Judas.

"Wait!" someone shouted.

Everyone turned to look outside the circle.

Soon, another came. "They want to stone Him."

"No, they cannot. Why would they stone a prophet, a Man of God?" a young girl asked, studying the leaders.

"High priest, what is this?" a man yelled.

"Murder!" another said, pointing at the stones.

"This cannot stand. There has been no trial," the onlookers said.

"What did He do?" a boy asked as he stood up.

The leaders stood there, staring at each other. The questions were enough, and they dropped their stones.

Rabbi went for the door, and just in time, Judas joined us. We made our way out.

Outside of the city, we returned to the Jordan. Though we sought refuge, the river more than anything reminded me there was nowhere we could hide. Rabbi knew what was ahead, yet He pursued it with boldness. I couldn't understand why His life was so worth giving up—or why the others did nothing.

Sighing, I knew he wouldn't avoid the opportunity to teach during the rest of the celebrations. I didn't know how many more times we would be able to escape. We didn't linger as we made our way to Jericho, and Rabbi continued teaching without hesitation.

"Rabbi!" I stared at the roof.

"John?" James called in a tired voice. "It's a dream. Go back to sleep."

Easy for him to say. He isn't being choked by nightmares. I balled up my tunic, wiped my face, and I looked around the quiet. Judas was gone. Sitting up, I kept watch.

A noise. I slammed into my mat, pretending to be asleep. The traitor crept back to his spot, quiet as a mouse. Glaring in his direction, I struggled to keep my eyes open.

Sunrise came. The sleepless nights had taken their toll. I could barely hold my eyes open as we walked out of town, scrunching my shoulder blades together to keep awake.

Andrew stopped ahead and waited for me to catch up to him. "Are you alive?" he asked with a squint. "You look like you could fall over. John?"

"I'm here."

"I see that but ... fine. The less you sleep, the harder it will be for you to let go. You can't control what comes next."

He walked ahead to the others, looking back at me with a shrug. Leaving Jericho was a relief. We made it through another town, but I wasn't' ready for what would come next. "Jericho, famed city, where Joshua exterminated the Canaanites," Simon began. "The war ..."

Something shuffled behind a tree. I leaned forward, focusing on the sycamore at the edge of the entrance. Silence. *Maybe Andrew was right.*

People entering the city stopped Rabbi, and He began to teach as we walked along. More shuffling—I whipped my head around at the noise—and locked eyes with Malchus. The head guard to the high priest had sunken eyes that were blocked by bushy eyebrows. He adjusted his blue hat, looking past me to Judas. He curled a fat finger, calling Judas to him.

I glared, daring Judas to go, and hurried to Peter. "Look, from the temple, he belongs to the high priest," I warned.

"Another guard. So what?" he said. "You see one every other minute. Leave me be. I am trying to listen—and you should too." Tapping his foot, he tried to draw Judas's attention.

I said, "Peter, this is something!"

"Quiet down—or go away. Those are your options!" Peter turned his attention back to Rabbi.

Two men sitting on the road shouted, "Master, have mercy on us! Mercy, Son of David!"

The crowd tried to hush them up, but they got all the louder, crying, "Master, have mercy on us! Mercy, Son of David!"

Rabbi stopped in front of them. "What do you want from Me?"

They said, "Master, we want our eyes opened. We want to see!"

Staring harder into their cloudy irises, I sensed despair. Rabbi must have felt it more. He went to them, ignoring the crowd and reached out, touching their eyes.

They had their sight back that very instant and joined the procession.

In my awe of His generosity, Malchus had taken the opportunity to slither to Judas. Behind him, he whispered in his ear. Moving through the crowd, I pushed eagerly, remembering the moment foreshadowed in my dream.

Malchus held his ground, blending into the growing crowd. He didn't seem to care I was close enough to hear their conversation.

"More mouths to feed. Money we don't have," Judas complained.

I hadn't heard him speak since my dream, but it was his normal voice, not the ominous growl I had heard that night.

Judas gripped our group's money sack, for which he was entrusted. "Luckily, I take what I can. Lest there be none left. No one appreciates the value of a coin; the cold metal between one's fingers gives a unique pleasure."

"Right you are. I know your story, Judas. What you've endured at the hands of your family," Malchus said.

"Family. They claimed to manage the best they could, but I could never be satisfied with so little," Judas said, clenching his teeth. "My father, devout man of God, took the little we had for offerings. He never cared for the precarious situations it caused. More often, we went to bed with empty bellies. Mother scolded us, reminding me daily that we were nothing more than mouths to feed and less for herself."

Malchus nudged him. "A burden. And now … all these people. The temple receives support from its followers, but who supports your Teacher, son?"

"No one."

He lied. A few of the local women, Mary, the one called Magdalene, from whom seven demons had gone out; Joanna, wife of Chuza, Herod's manager; and Susanna—along with many others who used their considerable means to provide.

"I can get you more," Malchus said. "The high priest is a generous man." Malchus placed his hand on Judas's shoulder. "He pays handsomely for information."

"*Information?*" he growled. Looking at me, he grated his teeth. The devil took him, invisible, except for the missing whites in his eyes.

"I only ask that you meet. He will answer all you request."

I pushed the man in front of me and hurried away. Too many people. They were gone.

CHAPTER FIFTEEN

lazarus

We went east to Bethany, which was where Mary and her sister Martha lived. They were friends, people we could trust. Their home had been a haven over the past three years, and I knew whatever plan was in place, Judas was outnumbered there. The village was on the crimson horizon, with the Mount of Olives at its back. I fixed my eyes on him, but Judas was back to normal—the darkness gone. I wondered why, but I had to keep moving.

"Master!" someone yelled, running toward us. "Master—he's—hurry."

Rabbi placed a hand on her shoulder.

Sighing, she said, "Master, the one you love so very much is sick."

Rabbi said, "This sickness is not fatal. It will become an occasion to show God's glory by glorifying God's Son."

Peter came to His side. "Rabbi, you can't do that. The Jews are out to kill You, and You're going back?"

"Are there not twelve hours of daylight? Anyone who walks in daylight doesn't stumble because there's plenty of light from the sun. Walking at night, he might very well stumble because he can't see where he's going. Our friend Lazarus has fallen asleep, but I am going there to wake him up."

Levi shook his head. "Master, if he's gone to sleep, he'll get a good rest and wake up feeling fine."

"Lazarus died, and I am glad for your sakes that I wasn't there. You're about to be given new grounds for believing. Now let's go to him."

Thaddaeus asked, "What about the leaders? They are waiting for us in Jerusalem—only two miles from Bethany."

James the lesser looked pale. "We won't survive another escape."

"It's too dangerous. It'll be the end of us," James added.

"We can fight. I've been through worse," Simon said.

James scoffed. "I doubt that. Most of us are unarmed."

"The perfect opportunity," Judas said with a ghost of a smile.

I staggered back toward Rabbi and stared at Judas blankly, waiting for the one who beckoned him to come forward.

Thomas gestured his hand like he held a sword. "Judas is right," he said. "Come along. We might as well die with Him."

They all agreed.

"John?" Peter asked.

I nodded quickly, trying to disguise my secret.

We didn't hurry to the village. Instead, we waited. I wasn't sure if Rabbi was afraid or if something more important called us to wait. Only He knew.

Two days later, we arrived outside Bethany. The rain trickled down on a group that was huddled together. Walking toward them, I heard agony and anger, and I saw sorrow. "You're too late, Rabbi. He's been in the tomb four days," a man said through his tears.

Lazarus was dead. It was obvious he had been loved, and many had come to comfort Martha and Mary. He had been funny and easy to talk to. I struggled as I looked into my own future if I failed to protect Rabbi. I felt awful at the thought of Abba and Mother mourning James and me. Even worse, I could picture Mother crying. I shook my head to clear my mind. There was no point in worrying about what hadn't happened.

Martha's dark lashes were clumped together with tears, touching the top of her round cheeks. She looked up with a brittle spirit. "Master, if You'd been here, my brother wouldn't have died. Even now, I know that whatever You ask God, He will give You."

Stepping gently toward her, Rabbi put her chin between His two fingers. "Your brother will be raised up."

Martha replied, "I know that he will be raised up in the resurrection at the end of time." Her eyes darted to the ground.

"You don't have to wait for the end. I am, right now, resurrection and life. The one who believes in Me, even though he or she dies, will live. And everyone who lives believing in Me does not ultimately die at all. Do you believe this?" He let go of her face.

Pinching the dribble under her nose, she cleared her throat. "Yes,

Master. All along, I have believed that You are the Messiah, the Son of God who comes into the world." She went to get her sister Mary.

When they returned, Mary stood at her side. Her brown eyes met mine as they came closer. She wasn't crying, but the dark circles under her eyes showed she had been. Though weary, she was still beautiful. She fell at His feet and said, "Master, if only You had been here, my brother would not have died."

He said, "Where did you put him?"

"Master, come and see," they said.

We followed them to Lazarus's tomb, which was not far down the way. It was a simple cave in the hillside with a slab of stone laid against it. Water pooled near its entrance.

Rabbi's brows drew together. He hesitated a moment, tracing the edge of the round door with His hand. His chin trembled, and He wept.

The twelve of us surrounded Him, and I put my hand on His shoulder as I had seen Him do many times.

Rabbi was courageous, furious at the guile of the leaders— joyful—extremely compassionate toward the suffering of others, but this time, He was hurt, saddened by the loss of His friend.

Those watching said, "Look how deeply He loved him."

Others said, "Well, if He loved him so much, why didn't He do something to keep him from dying? After all, He opened the eyes of a blind man."

Rabbi ignored the questions and said, "Remove the stone."

The sisters came to Rabbi, and Martha said, "Master, by this time, there's a stench. He's been dead four days!"

He looked her in the eye. "Didn't I tell you that if you believed, you would see the glory of God?" He turned to the others, and said "Go ahead, take away the stone."

Some of the men in the crowd came forward. Wide-eyed, they began to roll the stone away from the entrance. The wet warmth in the air carried out the smell of death. Lazarus's body was on a stone table.

Rabbi raised His eyes to heaven and prayed, "Father, I'm grateful that You have listened to Me. I know You always do listen, but on account of this crowd standing here, I've spoken so that they might believe that You sent Me." He shouted, "Lazarus, come out!"

Lazarus came out—a cadaver, wrapped from head to toe—with a kerchief over his face.

I froze.

Smiling, He said, "Unwrap him and let him loose."

Mary and Martha ran to Lazarus's side and embraced him.

"Oh, Lazarus!" Mary cried.

"Where am I?" he asked.

"You were dead! But now, you've been raised to newness of life!" Martha said as she hugged him.

I watched the empty tomb, and the crowd began to roar, celebrating the resurrection.

Rabbi and the twelve of us cheered, joining Mary and Martha at his side, but Judas was silent. Looking at Rabbi, he tapped his fingers on the outside of the money sack.

I didn't get it. He had all the reason in the world to be happy. There had been healings—people rid of possession long before His time. Perhaps even walking on the sea could be explained away as a ghost story, but this was like no other. No one had ever been raised from the dead. Nothing in the history of humanity could boast such a miracle, but Judas was numb to it.

The chanting and raving were only outmatched by the hundreds who soon came to check the truth of what had happened. Many more accepted Rabbi as the Son of God.

That night, we were all guests of Simon the Leper at the home of Lazarus, Mary, and Martha. We feasted on the warm flatbread, roasted meats, and bitter wine. Moments of peace, brought by only good friends, filled the night air. We celebrated Rabbi, but in the corner of my eye, I sensed the live version of my dream. It returned, and there was no way I would dismiss it as coincidence. I knew my dreams were real—and Satan was at the same table.

Mary came up to Rabbi, carrying an alabaster flask of nard. Opening the bottle, she poured it on His head.

Judas sat up on his knees. Pounding a fist on the table, he pressed it firmly into the wood. "That's criminal! A sheer waste! This perfume could have been sold for well over a year's wages and handed out to the poor." He pressed harder and harder into the table, and his eyes narrowed into slits.

"Let her alone. Why are you giving her a hard time? She has just done something wonderfully significant for Me. You will have the poor with you every day for the rest of your lives. Whenever you feel like it, you can do something for them. Not so with Me. She did what she could when she could—she pre-anointed My body for burial. And you can be sure that wherever in the whole world the Message is preached, what she just did is going to be talked about admiringly."

Burial?

Judas looked at his knuckles. "Oh. Look at that. Blood." He stood with an evil smile. "Rabbi, may I be excused?"

Rabbi agreed.

My eyes tracked Judas until he disappeared to the back room.

The next morning, the entire house packed up. Judas climbed down the stone steps outside the house, and we all waited for him.

"Did you sleep well, John?" he whispered.

I didn't say anything.

"What's with him? He seems happy, which is odd. Yesterday, he about lost it over the nard," James said to me as we walked along the road.

Thomas said, "Did you see his knuckles? Who would grind their own fist on an unfinished table?"

Andrew said, "Judas has always been off—and I know he takes money from the group. Peter said it's always short."

Peter came up behind us, adjusting the sack on his back. "Andrew, I told you to keep that to yourself. Yes, he steals, but he's only cheating himself. Leave it alone."

"Was stealing," Simon said, making sure Judas was too far away to hear.

Peter glared at him. "What do you mean *was?*"

Simon leaned in. "Ever since you mentioned he might be stealing ... and no, Peter this isn't the first time Andrew's mentioned it ... I started counting after he falls asleep."

"And?" Peter asked, looking him in the eye.

"I checked early this morning. There's extra. Thirty pieces of silver."

"Wait. That is way more than we were given." Peter stroked his beard.

James said, "He just needs a good punch to the gut. I'll set him on the right path."

I sighed. "That isn't going to do anything."

"He's cheating himself. Rabbi knows. Leave it alone." Peter hurried to Rabbi.

The rest of us stayed quiet. I think we had more to say, but none of us understood the idea of stealing. We had everything we needed. We were far from rich and had to rely on the kindness of His followers, but we never went without. Something about the silver bothered me. There was more to it, but I didn't know what. I felt the sharp prick of unwanted change in the pit of my gut, but there wasn't anything Rabbi didn't already know—so there was no point in getting upset. I hoped whatever Judas was planning wasn't going to be accomplished by holding a few coins.

Or was it?

We returned to Jerusalem on the first of the Days of Unleavened Bread.

Rabbi called to Andrew and me and said, "Go over to the village across from you. You'll find a donkey tethered there, her colt with her. Untie her and bring them to Me. If anyone asks what you're doing, say, 'The Master needs them!' He will send them with you."

So we went ahead of the others.

Entering the city, we saw a colt tied to a wooden post outside someone's home just as He had said.

"Here it is, John," Andrew said.

I looked down the road. "Let's get out of here before word gets to the leaders that we've come."

"He is the Son of God. He is protected ... *right?*" Andrew asked, untying the rope from the post.

"If you believe that, why are you hurrying?"

Wrapping the rope around his hands a few times, he secured the colt. "I'm not sure," he said after a moment.

I looked at the young donkey. The wilted little thing didn't seem prepared for his task—not unlike myself. "He's dirty," I said, removing my cloak. I thought about what lay ahead as the brisk morning air swept through my tunic. Draping my cloak across its back, I added, "We don't want Rabbi to be uncomfortable."

"He's so small. Will Rabbi fit?"

"It'll do."

Andrew placed his cloak on the colt, covering the rest of its back. "It will have to." He smiled. "Rabbi deserves some kindness, especially when we are about to enter the den of wolves."

We didn't make it five strides before someone shouted, "Thieves! What do you think you're doing with my colt?"

"What do we do, John?"

He halted, towering above me with a messed-up look on his face. "I asked you a question."

I wasn't sure if he was in support of Rabbi or loyal to the leaders. "Sir, the Lord needs them, and He will send them right away," I said, blinking.

"You are one of His?" he asked.

All I could see was hair creeping out of his tunic on top of huge muscles. One blow would send me and the colt flying.

Closer and closer. I closed an eye, hoping to survive.

Andrew's voice shook as he said, "We are."

He leaned over me. I swallowed a mouthful of spit and slid one foot behind me. James said it was the only way to fight someone bigger. If anything, I could charge his center—though it was wider than two of me.

"Take me to your Teacher!" he blurted, grabbing me at my sides. He lifted me from the ground. I couldn't move. Stiffening my everything, I braced myself as he swung me through the air. "I have wanted to meet Him for so long!"

I opened both eyes.

He set me down, patting me forcefully on the back. "You have no idea how I have prayed!" His eyes opened like a child.

I forced a smile, still unsure.

Andrew exhaled loudly.

"Can I follow you?" he asked again, raising his hands. "Jesus of Nazareth … here … riding my colt!"

"Yes, He is," Andrew said, signaling me to leave.

"Let us go to Him!" he said almost jumping. He was in tears, celebrating the mere thought of meeting Rabbi.

"This way," Andrew said, pointing down the road.

At the front of the city, Rabbi and the others were encircled by a crowd. Andrew led the colt to Him, and the crowd parted. Rabbi looked at the cloaks on its back and bowed His head to Andrew and me.

Peter and Thomas helped Him mount the donkey, and they led it by the rope into the city.

Nearly all the people in the crowd threw their garments down on the road, giving Him a royal welcome. Others cut branches from the trees and threw them down as a welcome mat. Crowds went ahead, and crowds followed, all of them calling out, "Hosanna to David's son! Blessed is He who comes in God's name! Hosanna in highest heaven!"

As He made His entrance into Jerusalem, the whole city was shaken. Unnerved, people asked, "What's going on here? Who is this?"

The parade crowd answered, "This is the prophet Jesus, the one from Nazareth in Galilee."

It was unlike anything I had ever seen.

Rabbi dismounted near the temple.

The man who followed and others approached Philip and said, "Sir, we want to see Jesus. Can you help us?"

"Who are you?"

"Greeks. We have traveled far. Come up to worship at the feast."

Philip went and told Andrew, and Andrew and Philip told Rabbi.

Rabbi answered, "Time's up. The time has come for the Son of Man to be glorified. Listen carefully: Unless a grain of wheat is buried in the ground, dead to the world, it is never any more than a grain of wheat, but if it is buried, it sprouts and reproduces itself many times over. In the same way, anyone who holds on to life just as it is destroys that life, but if you let it go, reckless in your love, you'll have it forever, real and eternal.

"If any of you wants to serve Me, then follow Me. Then you'll be where I am, ready to serve at a moment's notice. The Father will honor and reward anyone who serves Me. Right now, I am storm-tossed, but what am I going to say? 'Father, get Me out of this'? No, this is why I came in the first place. I'll say, 'Father, put your glory on display.'"

A voice came out of the sky: "I have glorified it—and I'll glorify it again!"

The crowd said, "Thunder!"

Others said, "An angel spoke to Him!"

Rabbi said, "The voice didn't come for Me but for you. At this moment, the world is in crisis. Now, Satan, the ruler of this world, will be thrown out. And I, as I am lifted up from the earth, will attract everyone to Me and gather them around Me." He put it this way to show how He was going to be put to death.

Voices from the crowd answered, "We heard from God's Law that the Messiah lasts forever. How can it be necessary, as You put it, that the Son of Man 'be lifted up'? Who is this 'Son of Man'?"

"For a brief time still, the light is among you. Walk by the light you have so darkness doesn't destroy you. If you walk in darkness, you don't know where you're going. As you have the light, believe in the light. Then the light will be within you and shining through your lives. You'll be children of light."

He went straight for the temple courts, and we followed Him inside.

CHAPTER SIXTEEN

betrayed

Inside, the halls were overcrowded with people making preparations for Passover. Custom required burnt animal sacrifices as atonement for wrongdoings be given to God—such had been done according to the ancient scrolls for hundreds of years. Tables were set up to exchange currencies from neighboring civilizations, enabling people to purchase animals and then hand them over for offering.

Rabbi's face was red, and the ridges bulging in His neck meant trouble. He pushed forward through the people. Scowling, He surveyed the temple, shuffling His line of sight across the room. I had never seen Him so upset.

He marched to the far end of the temple and placed his hands under the table of a money changer, staring at the man.

"Rabbi, how may I help you?" the man asked.

Baring His teeth, Rabbi lifted the table from the ground and flung it across the room. Coins flew, pinging on the cobbled floor. Rabbi ran wrathfully through the temple, turning over table after table. He grabbed a whip from the wall. Slinging it through the air, He chased out all who were buying and selling there. He kicked over the tables of loan sharks and the stalls of dove merchants. He quoted this text:

My house was designated a house of prayer;
You have made it a hangout for thieves.

There was hardly anyone left. Now there was room for the blind and crippled to get into the temple. They came to Him, and He healed them.

The children were running through the temple and shouting, "Hosanna to David's Son!"

The religious leaders were up in arms and took Him to task.

Shet said, "Do you hear what these children are saying?"

"Yes, I hear them. And haven't you read in God's Word, 'From the mouths of children and babies I'll furnish a place of praise'?"

Caiaphas's nostrils flared. "I know the teachings! Who *are* you?" he shouted.

Rabbi scoffed, but He didn't reply. He called us to follow Him, and we left.

Passover. It was time to make preparations for our celebratory meal. Custom called for it, but we didn't have anywhere to go. Who would risk our company? The twelve, except Peter, leaned on a wall, waiting for Rabbi near the gates of Jerusalem. We tried to pretend we weren't watching girls on the road as they entered. One came near, and I closed my eyes, swallowing up the sweet oil on her headdresses as she moved past me in the crowded passageway. Her clothed arm brushed against mine. I tried to smile at her, but I caught the stern scowl of her father and recanted. Girls kept their distance, which was perfect because we didn't smell nearly as good. The thought of any girl getting a whiff of my odor only made me sweat more.

"Why do they smell so good?" Andrew asked.

I inhaled again, taking in what lingered. "I don't know … what is it?"

"Lavender … I think," Andrew said, staring.

"Proper washing," James answered, lifting his head at a girl nearby. She giggled shyly.

"We never smell that good," Philip said, elbowing me.

"Not proper washing," I teased, smelling under my arm. I wasn't sure if her smell was real or imagined, but it excited me all the same.

"John! Andrew!" Peter shouted, waving his arms from across the crowd.

"Let's go. Peter's calling us," I said, pointing to him.

"I would rather stay here and see who else passes by," said Philip.

"Come. They will always be here." I grabbed his arm and pulled him across the line of people.

We made it over, and Peter said, "Rabbi needs you,"

Rabbi came outside the gate. He paused and called James and me, among the others, and said, "Go into the city. A man carrying a water jug will meet you. Follow him. Ask the owner of whichever house he enters, 'The Teacher wants to know, Where is my guest room where I can eat the Passover meal' … He will show you a spacious second-story room, swept and ready. Prepare for us there."

Peter came with us, and we went on our way doing all He asked.

That evening, after we finished the preparations, the twelve of us waited for Rabbi at a wooden table in the upper room. He entered the room barefoot. Walking toward us, He unlaced His belt and set it on a small table near the washing basin in the corner. Then He removed His cloak and took a towel resting on the basin and wrapped it around Him. He lifted the basin and bent over, filling it with water from a large drum.

He came to the table, smiling as He often did before something important happened. Setting the basin on the floor next to the table, He knelt in front of Peter.

Peter looked at Him and said, "Master, *You* wash my feet?"

"You don't understand now what I'm doing, but it will be clear enough to you later."

Peter said, "You're not going to wash my feet—ever!"

Rabbi reached for them again, and Peter slid his feet underneath him. "If I don't wash you, you can't be part of what I'm doing."

"Master!" said Peter. "Not only my feet then. Wash my hands! Wash my head!"

"If you've had a bath in the morning, you only need your feet washed now, and you're clean from head to toe. My concern, you understand, is holiness, not hygiene. So now you're clean, but not every one of you."

After He had finished washing, He took His robe, put it back on, and went back to His place at the table. "Do you understand what I have done to you? You address Me as 'Teacher' and 'Master,' and rightly so. That is what I am. So, if I, the Master and Teacher, washed your feet, you must now wash each other's feet. I've laid down a pattern for you. What I've done, you do. I'm only pointing out the obvious. A servant is not ranked above his master; an employee doesn't give orders to the employer. If you understand what I'm telling you, act like it—and live a blessed life. I'm not including all of you in this. I know precisely whom I've selected, so as not to interfere with the fulfillment of this scripture:

The one who ate bread at my table
Turned on his heel against me.

"I'm telling you all this ahead of time so that when it happens, you will believe that I am who I say I am. Make sure you get this right: Receiving someone I send is the same as receiving Me, just as receiving Me is the same as receiving the One who sent Me." He looked down at the table, shook His head, and looked up with a glare. "One of you is going to betray Me."

The others didn't say anything, looking around at one another and wondering who on earth He was talking about. I knew.

Rabbi reached for a piece of lamb. Holding it, He told the story of the first Passover. Generations ago, lambs were slain. Their blood was smeared across doorways, invoking God's protection over the Israelites as the angel of death was unleashed on all of Egypt, killing their firstborn sons. He set down the lamb and took a piece of bread.

Having taken and blessed the bread, He broke it and gave it to us. "Take, this is My body." Taking the chalice, He gave it and thanked God. "This is My blood, God's new covenant, poured out for many people. I'll not be drinking wine again until the new day when I drink it in the kingdom of God." He reclined in His seat.

We sank into our seats and moved on to the celebration.

I reclined against Him, resting my head on His shoulder. I wanted to blurt out what I knew, but my dreams were never proof enough for everyone else. I realized, despite all our time together, I hadn't shared my gift with Rabbi. It was foolish. I buried it, afraid to share with the One whom all gifts were given to. I opened my mouth, ready, but the words hung at the back of my throat. "Rabbi—"

Nathanael pounded on the table. Rabbi looked at him. He

shrugged into himself, downtrodden, gulping loudly. "Surely, You don't mean me, Lord? I—"

"Surely, You don't mean me, Lord?" Simon interrupted.

Soon, the others repeated the same.

Peter nudged me and whispered, *"You're closest. Ask Him."*

This is it. Time for the truth. Are my dreams a gift or a burden? I cleared my throat, turned to Him, and asked, "Master, who?"

"The one to whom I give this crust of bread after I've dipped it." Then He dipped the crust and gave it to Judas, son of Simon the Iscariot. As soon as the bread was in his hand, Satan entered him.

"What you must do," said Rabbi, "do. Do it and get it over with."

Satan and Judas were one again. They gripped the table, shot to their feet, and hurried out into the night.

I lifted up, ready to follow him, but Rabbi placed His hand over mine. I sat down.

"Now the Son of Man is seen for who He is, and God is seen for who He is in Him. The moment God is seen in Him, God's glory will be on display. In glorifying Him, He Himself is glorified—glory all around! Children, I am with you for only a short time longer. You are going to look high and low for Me, but just as I told the Israelites, I'm telling you: 'Where I go, you are not able to come.'"

Peter asked, "Master, just where are You going?"

"You can't now follow Me where I'm going. You will follow later."

"Master," said Peter, "why can't I follow now? I'll lay down my life for You!"

"Really? You'll lay down your life for Me? The truth is that before the rooster crows, you'll deny Me three times."

"Don't let this throw you. You trust God, don't you? Trust Me. There is plenty of room for you in My Father's home. If that weren't so, would I have told you that I'm on My way to get a room ready for you? And if I'm on My way to get your room ready, I'll come back and get you so you can live where I live. And you already know the road I'm taking."

Thomas said, "Master, we have no idea where You're going. How do You expect us to know the road?"

"I am the Road, also the Truth, also the Life. No one gets to the Father apart from Me. If you really knew Me, you would know My Father as well. From now on, you do know Him. You've even seen Him!"

Philip said, "Master, show us the Father—and then we'll be content."

"You've been with Me all this time, Philip, and you still don't understand? To see Me is to see the Father. So how can you ask, 'Where is the Father?' Don't you believe that I am in the Father and the Father is in Me? The words I speak to you aren't mere words. I don't just make them up on My own. The Father who resides in Me crafts each word into a divine act.

"Believe Me: I am in My Father, and My Father is in Me. If you can't believe that, believe what you see—these works. The person who trusts Me will not only do what I'm doing but even greater things, because I, on My way to the Father, am giving you the same work to do that I've been doing. You can count on it. From now on, whatever you request along the lines of who I am and what I am doing, I'll do it. That's how the Father will be seen for who He is in the Son. I mean it. Whatever you request in this way, I'll do.

"If you love Me, show it by doing what I've told you. I will talk to the Father, and He'll provide you another Friend so that you will always have someone with you. This Friend is the Spirit of Truth. The godless world can't take Him in because it doesn't have eyes to see Him, doesn't know what to look for, but you know Him already because He has been staying with you—and He will even be *in* you!

"I will not leave you orphaned. I'm coming back. In just a little while, the world will no longer see Me, but you're going to see Me because I am alive—and you're about to come alive. At that moment, you will know absolutely that I'm in My Father, and you're in Me, and I'm in you.

"The person who knows My commandments and keeps them, that's who loves Me. And the person who loves Me will be loved by My Father, and I will love him and make Myself plain to him."

Thaddeus said, "Master, why is it that You are about to make Yourself plain to us but not to the world?"

"Because a loveless world," said Rabbi, "is a sightless world. If anyone loves Me, he will carefully keep My word, and My Father will love him. We'll move right into the neighborhood! Not loving Me means not keeping My words. The message you are hearing isn't Mine. It's the message of the Father who sent Me.

"I'm telling you these things while I'm still living with you. The Friend, the Holy Spirit whom the Father will send at My request, will make everything plain to you. He will remind you of all the things I have told you. I'm leaving you well and whole. That's My parting gift to you. Peace. I don't leave you the way you're used to being left—feeling abandoned, bereft—so, don't be upset. Don't be distraught.

"You've heard Me tell you, 'I'm going away, and I'm coming back.' If you loved Me, you would be glad that I'm on My way to the Father because the Father is the goal and purpose of My life.

"I've told you this ahead of time, before it happens, so that when it does happen, the confirmation will deepen your belief in Me. I'll not be talking with you much more like this because the chief of this godless world is about to attack, but don't worry—he has nothing on Me, no claim on Me, but so the world might know how thoroughly I love the Father, I am carrying out My Father's instructions right down to the last detail. Get up. Let's go. It's time to leave here."

He led us over the brook Kidron at a place where there was a garden, called Gethsemane. He called Peter, James, and me to accompany

Him into the heart of the garden. "Stay here while I go over there and pray."

He paced back and forth, scanning the empty garden, and then He placed a hand against the trunk of an olive tree. "I feel bad enough right now to die. Stay here and keep vigil with Me."

Going a little ahead, He fell to the ground and prayed for a way out: "Papa, Father, You can—can't You?—get Me out of this. Take this cup away from Me, but please, not what I want—what do You want?"

What cup?

I saw His face in the moonlight—His brow wrinkled—eyes shut in prayer. I could hear as He inhaled and exhaled, sounding deeply troubled.

The night drew on. The three of us sat silent under one of the trees. I tried moving around to keep from falling asleep.

His words woke us. "Can't you stick it out with Me a single hour? Stay alert; be in prayer so you don't wander into temptation without even knowing you're in danger. There is a part of you that is eager, ready for anything in God, but there's another part that's as lazy as an old dog sleeping by the fire."

I couldn't believe I fell asleep. Between the chunks of lamb resting in my belly and the darkness in my friend, it was too much, but I wouldn't fall asleep again. He needed me.

He left a second time. Again, He prayed, "My Father, if there is no other way than this, drinking this cup to the dregs, I'm ready. Do it Your way."

My head felt like stone. I moved my shoulders up and down, anything to stay awake. I thought about standing and walking around, but I didn't.

"Are you going to sleep all night? No—you've slept long enough. Time's up. The Son of Man is about to be betrayed into the hands of sinners. Get up. Let's get going. My betrayer has arrived."

Too late.

CHAPTER SEVENTEEN

a dark night

We were trapped. Malchus—his men, imperial soldiers and their commander-readied swords, clubs, and shields—stood with His betrayer, Judas. I wasn't sure what vile lies the high priest had used to coax the Romans to their sides, but as Judas pushed forward carrying a lantern to the center of the circle, I prepared myself.

Rabbi went toward them. "Who are you after?"

They answered, "Jesus the Nazarene."

"I Am."

As soon as He said it, they fell backward on the ground, forced into submission, leaving only His betrayer and the shadow behind Him.

Judas stood there like a puppet on strings held up by something doomed from the other side.

Again, Rabbi asked, "Who are you after?"

They stood, grabbed their weapons, and said, "Jesus the Nazarene."

Judas went straight to Rabbi and said, "How are You, Rabbi?" Leaning in, he kissed Him on the cheek. Judas's lip split open, and he grabbed his mouth. Touching it in disbelief, his eyes widened.

I didn't care who Judas was with, I went for him—but James snatched my arm, squeezing it with both hands.

Rabbi shook His head. "Judas, you would betray the Son of Man with a kiss?" He looked at the armed men and asked, "Friend, why this charade? I'm the One. So, if it's Me you're after, let these others go."

Charging, they grabbed Rabbi's arms and twisted them behind His back.

James held tight, and I tried to pry my arm free.

Peter ran toward them. Pulling his own sword from its sheath, he drew it and shouted, "Master, shall we fight?"

With my free hand, I slapped James across the face.

He flinched, letting go. "No, John!" he screamed.

I ran toward one of the soldiers and went for his sword, ducking underneath his swing. I could hear it pierce the air, narrowly losing my head. I jumped back, waiting for an opening. The Roman soldier's training was far above any Israelite. I couldn't get close.

I turned behind me. Peter swung the blade through the air, slicing off Malchus's ear.

Malchus gripped his face and screamed, "Ah! Help! Seize him!" He fell, staring at the ear on the ground. Wailing in horror, he yelled, "Kill … kill Him! I … I am the serv … servant of the high … highest priest … priestess!"

Judas gasped and ran out of the garden with his hand to his lips.

The other guards drew their swords and moved toward Peter.

Rabbi called out Peter's name. "Let them be. Even in this." Then He said, "Put your sword back where it belongs. All who use swords are destroyed by swords. Don't you realize that I am able right now to call to My Father, and twelve companies—more, if I want them— of fighting angels would be here, battle ready? But if I did that, how would the scriptures come true that say this is the way it has to be?"

Peter flung his sword to the ground with a subdued glare.

Rabbi walked over to Malchus, cupped his wound in His hand, and healed it.

Malchus rose, touching his full ear again and again.

Rabbi looked at the guards and said, "What is this—coming out after Me with swords and clubs as if I were a dangerous criminal? Day after day, I have been sitting in the temple, teaching, and you never so much as lifted a hand against Me." Then He walked to them. "But do it your way—it's a dark night, a dark hour."

"Take Him," Malchus instructed.

They bound Him with rope. Pushing Him to walk, they marched away.

I fell to my knees. "Rabbi!" I called.

He said nothing, going with them.

I called out to God, "Stop them! Protect Him!"

The rest of the guards moved toward the three of us.

Peter put up his hands, turned, and darted out of the garden.

James took a step back as the guards moved closer. He grabbed my arm, dragged me to the ground, and ran. My feet flailed about against the roots of olive trees, and all I could do was cry out, "God, send Your legion of angels. Don't leave Him! Don't let them take Rabbi!"

A few miles outside the garden, I sat and stared at my torn arms and legs. "We just left Him!"

James was bent over. "What … did … you … say?"

I shot up, pushing him down with all that was in me. "What have you done?" I shouted.

He got up and charged me. "What have *I* done?"

We collided and I fell backward, hitting my head.

"What I've done is save your life!" he said.

"I don't have time for this," I said, standing up. "All we've ever done is fight. And for what? *Nothing*! You fight for everything, but why not for Him?"

"I did—didn't want—"

"Want what? To help? To save His life?"

"No, I did want to help. I didn't want to die!" He looked at me. I could see it in his eyes. The fear. It wasn't his fault. I felt the weight, but I couldn't leave Rabbi. I had to try something. I couldn't sit around waiting for someone older or stronger. There was no time. I had to help Him. I turned and ran away.

Within moments, I came to where He was taken, but no one was there. I knew exactly where they were headed.

Blackness filled the empty streets, except for a single light in the high priest's courtyard. Running farther, I crept toward it.

"*John?*" a voice called. I turned behind me. It was Annas. "What are you doing here at this hour?"

I said nothing.

"You followed Him, did you not? And there," he pointed behind me, "another follower of His."

I whipped my head around, cautious of the traitor. Instead, I saw Peter with the high priest's servants warming himself at a fire. *What is he doing?*

"Come inside, John. It's cold out here." He stepped aside, gesturing farther into the lion's den.

I'm not afraid. I won't hide.

Annas pointed to a spot near the outer wall. "Wait here."

They dragged Rabbi to Annas. I wanted to go to Him, but He was surrounded.

Annas said, "It's over. What You do from here will decide Your fate. What say You?"

"I've spoken openly in public. I've taught regularly in meeting places and the temple. Everything has been out in the open. I've said nothing in secret. So why are You treating Me like a conspirator? Question those who have been listening to Me. They know well what I have said. My teachings have all been aboveboard."

One of the guards slapped Him. "How dare you!."

"If I've said something wrong, prove it, but if I've spoken the plain truth, why this slapping around?"

"Take Him to my son-in-law," Annas instructed.

Then Annas sent Him, still tied up, to the chief priest.

I followed, clinging to the shadows, to the inner room. I could see Him at the center of the Sanhedrin. The seventy-one elect surrounded Him like vultures waiting to devour a single bone. I held my breath, wanting to hear every word.

Caiaphas was silent, staring at me.

Zedekiah came forward and said, "I will tell you why we have called you from your homes. You have all heard the stories, seen the lies with your own eyes. Tonight, I have witnesses who can confirm that Jesus of Nazareth calls Himself the Son of God while possessed by a demon." He shoved an old man forward.

Stumbling, the old man pointed at Rabbi. "Yes, Your Honors, it is so. He is possessed and claims to be God Himself!"

Shet said, "I saw Him offer to pay this woman, so she might claim He healed her. Come, tell them what you told me."

An old woman, covering her face with her shawl, said, "Yes, I was never ill, but I used His payment in dedication to the temple."

I had never seen either of them, and I had been at His side for three years.

Plenty of people were willing to bring up false charges, but nothing added up, and they ended up canceling each other out. Two more came forward. "We heard Him say, 'I am going to tear down this temple, built by hard labor, and in three days build another without lifting a hand.'" But even they couldn't agree exactly.

Caiaphas stood up before them and walked over to Rabbi. "Are You not going to answer? What is this testimony that these men are bringing against You?"

I bit my lip, waiting for Rabbi to undo their claims as He had done before, but He said nothing.

"Are You the Messiah, the Son of the Blessed One?" Caiaphas demanded.

"Yes, I am, and you'll see it yourself: 'The Son of Man seated at the right hand of the Mighty One, arriving on the clouds of heaven'."

Caiaphas's eyes bulged. Ripping his clothes, he yelled, "Did you hear that? After that, do we need witnesses? You heard the blasphemy. Are you going to stand for it?"

Josephus pushed to the center and slapped Him. "He is worthy of death!"

"He must die!" Zedekiah shouted.

Shet spat from where he stood. "Death!" he yelled.

I watched as more spat at Him. They blindfolded His eyes.

Caiaphas hit Him and said, "Who hit You? Prophesy!"

The guards, punching and slapping, took Him away.

I stood alone. I didn't know what to do or where they were taking Him. I knew I couldn't follow.

"You!" someone shouted near the courtyard.

My eyes followed the sound. *Peter!*

A servant girl pointed at him. "You were with the Nazarene, Jesus."

He denied it: "I don't know what you're talking about." He went out on the porch, and a rooster crowed.

I followed him, hiding in the shadows.

She flagged the guards over. "Here!" she shouted.

They gathered so quickly that I couldn't make my way to him.

The girl spotted him and said, "He's one of them."

He denied it again. "You've got to be one of them. You've got 'Galilean' written all over you."

"I never laid eyes on this Man you're talking about." Just then, the rooster crowed a second time. He ran down the street.

I tried to follow him, but I couldn't keep up. *Why didn't they come after me? Why did he lie? Maybe he was right to be afraid.*

I hid, avoiding those leaving the high priest's home. When I reached the city gates, I saw endless nothing. We were all separated. *How did everything get so messed up?* I plopped down under a tree, trying not to fall asleep, but I did.

In my dream, I saw a great fire. Burning red and orange, it consumed the world and all in it. Trees turned to dust in seconds, animals and people scurried, trying to flee certain death, but one alone stood firm. His silhouette, unflinching to the frenzy, was unscathed. He alone survived, calling others out by name. I woke to the vague uncertainty of a new day.

A rattling nearby. I hurried, hiding behind the trunk.

Judas? Of all the unholy coincidences.

I crawled forward, studying him. "Traitor," I mumbled.

He didn't notice me. He didn't seem to notice anything. He held something at his side, studying a row of trees near the city gates.

Rope?

Then he stood in front of the largest one. Muttering, he traced his hand along a sturdy branch just out of reach. In the silence, I could hear his words. "I've sinned. I've betrayed an innocent Man." He flung the rope across the branch and looped the end of the rope around his neck. He scaled the tree, looking up to the sky with a hollow expression.

I clamored to my feet. Unsteady, I tried to hurry to him, but he let go, hanging. His body shook, flinging through the air. I was too late. He drew his last breath, staring forward as if something insidious received him on the other side.

I looked away. I never wanted any of it. *If only I had been nicer. If only I had followed him when he was with Malchus. If only …*

I turned, looking at him again. "Rabbi," I said. There was no way I would leave Him to share the same fate: to die alone.

CHAPTER EIGHTEEN

pilate

The best way to find Rabbi was to find the crowd. I could hear the sound of my own heart as I ran back into town. Every next moment seemed to be filled with regret and confusion. Judas's swinging body pushed me to run faster than I ever had. There they were, gathered outside the praetorium of the fortress of Antonia, military barracks of the governor.

I had never seen it surrounded by rioters. Such a thing would have demanded the forces of Rome seize the entire city, but something or someone had diminished the need for status. I pushed through the dense crowd and beheld the most powerful man in all Judea: Pontius Pilate.

Marcus Pontius Pilate. The prefect, governor of Judea, was trying to speak above the chaos. The sun snuck over the horizon as if it too were afraid of the uproar. He scratched through his Roman hairstyle, cut blunt around a squared brow. He glared at the people with discerning black eyes and wrinkled his pointed nose, trying to hear.

"What charge do you bring against this Man?"

He roared, "One at a time! I cannot hear you, savages, through your ranting and raving! One at a time!" he demanded. "You, there," he said, pressing his tiny top lip into his larger bottom one. "Are you not the leader? Why have you come—and tell me why I should not have you all removed from this place at once!"

Yet they continued shouting until Caiaphas's slithering through the people inflicted a deathly silence. "We found this Man undermining our law and order, forbidding taxes to be paid to Caesar, setting himself up as Messiah-King."

More lies. He knows the governor can't allow opposition to Caesar.

"We have sat silent since your appointment since you began filling our Jerusalem with pagan symbols on coins and statues. In times past, we revolted, used violence, but now we ask for unity. We ask you to join us in silencing this false prophet."

Pilate shifted his incredulous stare to Rabbi. "Is this true that You're 'King of the Jews'?"

I tried to move so I could see Him, to tell Him He wasn't alone, but no one would let me through.

"Those are your words, not Mine."

They shoved Him closer to the stone steps where Pilate stood, heavily guarded. "I find nothing wrong here. He seems harmless enough to me." Pilate turned to leave.

"No!" Caiaphas shouted.

The crowd froze. Maybe he had lost his mind, but everyone knew you couldn't yell at the prefect.

Caiaphas adjusted his shawl and lowered his voice, saying, "If He hadn't been doing something evil, do you think we'd be here bothering you?"

"You take Him. Judge Him by *your* law."

Caiaphas hit his cane on the steps. "We're not allowed to kill anyone."

Zedekiah came forward, standing next to the high priest. "He's stirring up unrest among the people with His teaching, disturbing the peace everywhere, starting in Galilee and now all through Judea. He's a dangerous Man, endangering the peace."

"Prefect, you *need* to avoid further disruptions in your lands," Caiaphas said. "Will those above you allow this constant chaos, constant discourse?"

Pilate glared at them, and then he shook his head. "So He's a Galilean?"

"He is, Prefect," Shet answered, moving in.

"Take Him to Herod—for this is his matter," he said, dismissing the mob.

In one sentence, Pilate bought Rabbi more time, but at the same time, he sent Him to the man who had ordered the Baptizer's head on a platter.

The leaders made way to King Herod. Shoving Rabbi, they scaled the steps of his home, which was covered with carvings and statues. I had waited for what seemed like forever to look the king in the face. Part of me imagined storming into his home, walking up to him, and punching him in the jaw—and then grabbing him by the throat to tell him he had murdered an innocent man—but it was just as impossible as doing something now. The only being who could save Rabbi was God Himself.

The guards outside went in, and there he was. He looked too young to be in charge of a quarter of Galilee. He examined the mob with the doting eyes of a lamb and dumb ears that made his head look too small. Every strand of his hair was combed toward his face as all Romans did. He came down the steps, adjusting heavy plates of gold and silver on his chest. No doubt as co-tetrarch with his brother Philip, he had the finest luxuries, even his face on our coins. It didn't seem like he had any need to kill the Baptizer—or anyone else for that matter. I hoped he could see that now. "Why have you called an audience with me?" The king glared down at Caiaphas, Shet, and Zedekiah from his raised seat.

Caiaphas said, "As one of us, here for Passover, we know you will take more action than Pilate. He refuses—"

"Are you on a first-name basis with the prefect? You forget your place, High Priest," he said.

Caiaphas glared at him. "Since when do you care for how we address your competitor?"

"Competitor? Our feud is none of your concern. Though, by the state of things, I think you will use it to your favor." He grinned like a wolf in a sheep pen.

"We know you are not a fan of the prefect, which is clear by your hiding within your quarters," Caiaphas said.

"The matter is no longer your concern. I will not repeat myself a second time, High Priest."

No longer? What have you been up to?

For a moment, the high priest looked desperate. His jaw thrust forward. "Well, you and your new wife—who once belonged another—have enjoyed the lavish home reserved for only Roman authorities, but do not forget your people."

"*My* people? We've discussed this already," he said.

"The people gathered here are only a small fraction of those who know of your recent separation from the Nabataean king, Aretas IV's, daughter. But—"

"But what can be done? The matter is settled," the king said.

"Yes, well the people will not be as confident in your decision to rid yourself of your wife for *your half brother's* wife. As you well know, such a thing is offensive to many."

Zedekiah stepped forward and said, "King Herod, unfortunately, the people will not overlook another grievance from you, and we fear you will lose control of our portion of your father's beloved kingdom."

"Is that so?"

"Yes, it is!" Caiaphas said. "We know you cannot suffer another interruption in these lands as you did in your recent loss."

"Loss?"

"We know of the border war with the Nabataean people caused by your indiscretion. We *know* you have done everything to avoid another mishap. We also know of what became of the Baptizer and the real reason why he is no longer with us," he said, glaring at the king.

"We agreed we wouldn't speak—"

"Agreements have contingencies, and here stands another instigator, agitator to our people!"

"Fine. Bring Him."

The crowd parted. Herod beheld Rabbi and smiled like a child receiving his first toy. "This Man? He is the Miracle Worker? Closer," he said, gesturing for the guards to bring Him. "I have waited a long time. I've heard so much about You. Show me. Show what You can do."

Rabbi said nothing.

"Show me that You can heal—You can call demons."

Still nothing.

Why Rabbi? Why not gain his favor? Impress him. Why won't You answer?

"Can You not do all that the stories say? Perform some sort of sign?" he asked, sitting on the edge of his seat. "Is it true You heal the blind and lame? I've heard reports You even walked across the sea?"

Rabbi stood there silent.

The king's face shifted from a grin to a curled upper lip.

"You see, this Man claims to be the king of us all," Caiaphas said.

"A king?" a soldier said, interrupting in laughter. "Is He a king in torn robes and hands tied?"

"I will help Him become what He claims," another soldier said. He went into Herod's quarters, came back with a piece of fine fabric, and approached Rabbi. They slung it across His back, dressing Him up in a king's costume.

Herod laughed at their display. "I see no cause to be involved in this matter."

"But, King Herod," Caiaphas said.

"I have done enough on your behalf—or have you forgotten? I will not be your *puppet* again, High Priest." He dismissed them.

We hurried back to the prefect, and I could hear their scheming.

"We must take this more seriously, lest our celebrations be inhibited by this agitator," Caiaphas hollered.

"How much more can we do?"

"I will show you, Zedekiah. I will show you!" Caiaphas said.

Caiaphas began to grab people along their way, whispering, "You must join us and be rid of this Jesus of Nazareth. He is a danger to our people." To another group standing along our way, he said, "You will lose your place in the temple if you do not support our cause. God wills us to end the tirade of any blasphemer."

Over and over, he called, and the crowd tripled.

I was pushed further behind. I couldn't believe the number of people who joined, submitting to his bullying. I knew many faces in the crowd—some who just the day before shouted "Hosanna" to him—people Rabbi had been kind and loving to. He had only ever wanted for them to come as they were, but they quickly disregarded His teachings to protect their places in the synagogue.

When we were back at the praetorium, they scaled the steps over the shrill crowd.

Pilate called in the high priests, rulers, and others and said, "You brought this Man to me as a disturber of the peace. I examined Him in front of all of you and found there was nothing to your charge. And neither did Herod, for he has sent Him back here with a clean bill of health. It's clear that He's done nothing wrong, let alone anything deserving death. I'm going to warn Him to watch His step and let Him go."

The crowd began to roar, "No! No! No!"

Caiaphas stretched his hand across the people and said, "These people gathered will not stand for His release. He claims to be King—and He opposes Caesar."

Pilate said, "Aren't You going to answer anything? That's quite a list of accusations."

Still, He said nothing.

Pilate looked at the people gathered and added, "I will punish Him. Scourge Him!"

The soldiers took Rabbi into the praetorium.

Pushing my way through, I tried to hurry. I knew the horror of Roman scourging, forbidden to any Roman and reserved only for the forgotten. Covered in sweat, I broke through the people, hiding between the prefect's home and the prison. I lifted myself to a barred window carved in stone. There He was, standing with His hands tied above Him in only His loincloth.

The soldier chosen to scourge Him stood in front of Him with a devilish grin. Abba warned us the Romans relished in any opportunity to humiliate or inflict pain on our people, but watching him circle Rabbi, while holding a flagrum, I could see they were beyond cruel.

My stomach sprung at the leather rod wrapped in rope—split into six strands, three feet in length. The sun glistened over the metal ball bearings at the end of the strands as the soldier lifted it to Rabbi's face. He pricked his finger on the animal bone woven within, winking.

The thought of what the jagged pieces would do to His flesh made the bitter liquid inside my stomach fill my mouth. I swallowed, refusing to give the vile soldier what he wanted but wasn't getting out of Rabbi. I didn't realize my grip on the wall was so firm that when I tried to ease off it, I nearly fell to my knees. I wished I could look Rabbi in the eyes and let Him know He wasn't alone.

He began. Sending the weighted throngs through the air, he grinned. A high-pitched whistling sliced the silence—metal and rope pounded the layers of His skin, softening it for the animal bone. The pieces wedged, hidden within His flesh. The soldier thrashed the flagrum upward ripping it from His back, exposing muscle—blood spewed—over the flagrum, Rabbi's back, and the soldier's face. The soldier spat the blood out, unbothered, and kept on.

My head swayed in a small circle as I tried to imagine the excruciating pain. Every smash made me wince in horror. I couldn't bear it, and my stomach emptied yellow slosh onto my sandals.

The soldier continued blow after blow, over and over. Each connection ripped more flesh from His back and legs. Then I saw Him, through a flood of tears, as He slumped over.

A brood of soldiers hoisted him back to a standing position—to assist them in further damaging His body.

The flagrum wrapped around His waist and chest, removing more flesh. It held pieces, boasting its effectiveness as a weapon of extreme torture. The remaining flesh hung in strips from His back.

My knees buckled as I saw His swollen face. He was unrecognizable. His eyes fused shut. The cuts were everywhere, and He was drenched in blood. I could hear whispers of His faint breaths through the shrieking of the flagrum. Again and again, he whipped Him.

Why won't they stop?

Israelites forbade more than forty lashes, but the Romans clearly saw no reason for such a limit. They continued mercilessly.

His body rested, knees bent. The soldier finally stopped from his own exhaustion. Rabbi looked dead. I watched, fixing my eyes to His chest—waiting.

Then, He inhaled filling His lungs with a burst of nourishment.

The soldiers untied His hands, allowing Him to collapse onto the stone pavement. He laid there, in a growing pool of His blood, shattered.

The Roman soldiers had not had their fill. They dragged Him into the praetorium and gathered the whole company of soldiers around Him.

I shivered, terrified of what would happen next.

One soldier lifted Him, paying no mind to His gaping flesh. "Look," he mocked, "hail to the King. Go get Him a crown!"

A soldier ran to a garden shrub decorating the wall of the praetorium, grabbed a thorn vine, and winced as he plaited it into a crown. Running back, he shoved the crown over Rabbi's brow and head. The thorns pierced His face, adding to His agony and suffering.

Another centurion fetched a scarlet robe from within and draped it over His torn flesh.

I didn't know why they needed to add to their cruelty with humiliation.

They surrounded Him and spit on Him. Taunting Him, they chortled, "King of the Israelites!" To add to their joke, they handed Him a stick, pretending it was a royal scepter.

When He couldn't hold it, they removed it from His loose grip and used it to beat the crown of thorns into His head, forcing it deeper and deeper into His flesh.

Blood poured into His eyes, but Rabbi was silent. I couldn't tell if He was dead—if they were now just taunting His corpse. I didn't know how anyone could survive such heinous treatment. My mouth filled again, and I couldn't hold it in.

The monsters ripped the robe that stuck to His back. The sticky, clotted barrier was torn callously from His wounds, and then they forcefully put back on His clothes.

I rocked back and forth. I couldn't take any more of the relentless torture. I caved. Falling to my knees, I sobbed. Unable to catch my breath, I let go. I let the fear in. I was ready to die from the sorrow of what I had witnessed. I swallowed, trying to grip reality and thinking of His strength on the other side of the wall. He had lasted longer than anyone else would have.

A hand gripped my shoulder. The firmness reminded me of Rabbi, always at my side in times of stress and confusion. I looked up, and I saw Him. He was smiling, but His smile drifted away, resting at the wrinkles of a distraught face. *Mary?*

"John, my son," she said.

I wasn't alone.

Another voice behind me. "John, John! We found you! You survived. Stand, son."

"*Mother?*" She knelt next to me and squeezed me nearly in half.

I fell apart. I couldn't speak. I couldn't tell her all that she needed to know. He was gone now, but I couldn't say the words.

They helped me to my feet, and we stood there in silence. I realized they had seen everything too. My heart cried out to Mary.

"He is still alive!" a solider shouted.

I whipped myself out of their arms and ran to the window. There He was—alive. He had survived. I wiped my face, huffing. All I needed to do was get Him home, and everything would be fine again.

The solider who whipped Him looked Him over and said, "Take Him to Pilate!"

Other soldiers dragged Him half alive to Pilate's doors, and we followed.

Coming out, Pilate appealed to the leaders again. "He will forever bear the scars of His torture and cannot claim to be king."

Everyone was afraid of how He looked.

"I present Him to you, but I want you to know that I do not find Him guilty of any crime."

When the high priests and police saw Him, they shouted, "Crucify! Crucify!"

Pilate said, "You take Him. You crucify Him. I find nothing wrong with Him."

Caiaphas ordered, "We have a law, and by that law, He must die because He claimed to be the Son of God."

Pilate tried his best to pardon Him, but they shouted him down: "If you pardon this Man, you're no friend of Caesar's. Anyone setting himself up as 'king' defies Caesar."

Zedekiah balled his fist, calling the crowd to join him. "Kill Him!"

Pilate said, "Here is your king."

They shouted back, "Kill Him! Kill Him! Crucify Him!"

Pilate said, "I am to crucify your *king*?"

The high priest answered, "We have no king except Caesar."

CHAPTER NINETEEN

the cross

Pilate caved to their demand and turned Him over to be crucified.
The soldiers forced Rabbi out of the praetorium and down the street
to the shouts of, "Die! Die!"

I stumbled, trying to hurry with Mother, Mary, the other Mary—the mother of Clopas—and Mary Magdalene close behind. Soon more who loved Him joined. He wasn't alone, but there was nothing we could do.

To the hill of Golgotha, place of the skull, we followed. The Romans insisted He drag His own instrument of death—a cross. He had little life in Him and struggled to carry the weight of the rugged cypress tree across His tattered shoulder uphill.

I got close enough to yell. "Rabbi, we're here! You're not alone!"

However, He didn't turn to me. Maybe He couldn't.

Behind me, I heard Mary wailing. I turned to her hollow expression right as she fell. Running to her, I helped her up and steadied her in my arms. She buckled again. I could only brace her fall. On her knees, she cried out, "Abba, please be with Him!"

Mary Magdalene came up behind us. "We must go on," she said, pressing Mary into her side.

Ahead, Rabbi fell forward—still as death—and the crowd stopped. He coughed and squirmed under the cross, trying to lift Himself, but His legs couldn't bear the weight.

The Marys whimpered as He struggled to get up. Mary Magdalene reached out for Him and wailed, "Rabbi!"

He looked in our direction with a swollen face. "Daughters of Jerusalem, don't cry for Me. Cry for yourselves and for your children. The time is coming when they'll say, 'Lucky the women who never conceived! Lucky the wombs that never gave birth! Lucky the breasts that never gave milk!' Then they'll start calling to the mountains, 'Fall down on us!' calling to the hills, 'Cover us up!' If people do these things to a live, green tree, can you imagine what they'll do with deadwood?" He gripped the ground beneath Him and stood up. Like a leaf seconds from being carried off by the wind, He continued uphill.

The heavy crossbar slid across His back, and He fidgeted again and again. Without water, the rising sun delivered the second beating. He slowed. There was no help. The blood that spilled from

Him left a ghost of a person. He collapsed, and the weighted cross collided into His tired body.

Mary and I ran to Him. Before we reached the street, someone shouted, "Get back, you, or I'll slice the both of you in half!" We halted, staring at his twisted face. "Get up, now!" he roared.

Another one bent next to Rabbi and grappled His arm, slipping. He wiped the blood on the cloth he pulled from his armor. "You, come." He gestured to a man in the crowd. "What is your name?"

"Me?" he looked around. "I don't want trouble, sir."

"Well, you've found it anyway. Your name!"

"Simon, sir. My name is Simon," he stuttered, hands up.

"Simon? You don't look like one of them. Where are you from? Do you support Him?"

"I am from Cyrene. I have heard stories, but I do not know Him."

"Cyrene … a distant land." The soldier laughed. "Have you come to see Him killed?"

"No, no, sir. I was passing on my way to the countryside when I saw Him." Simon looked at Rabbi.

"Help Him," the soldier demanded.

Simon nodded and ran to Rabbi's side. Bending down, he wrestled the cross, lifted it, and rested it across his right shoulder. With his free hand, he reached out for Rabbi. Rabbi took his hand and hobbled to His feet. Both continued walking in stride. We followed, tracing the edge of the road.

"Rabbi, I'm here. I won't leave you. You're not alone," I called to Him.

He didn't make one sound. No wailing. No complaints. Silent in His task ahead.

I wiped my face and took a deep breath, trying very hard to be like Him.

Why, Rabbi? Why? Why don't you run? Why don't You call Your angels to Your side? Why leave willingly? Why accept this sentence? You've done nothing wrong.

At the top of Golgotha, the sun hung with fading light, unaware it was morning. The soldiers wasted no time. Ripping the cross from Rabbi and Simon, they threw it to the ground. Rabbi fell. Two soldiers bent down and flipped Him on His back. They stripped Him, leaving Him in only His loincloth. I balled my fist. I could have run to Him and done something, but I didn't know how.

They dragged His limp body, placing Him on top of the cross. Kneeling at each side of the crossbar, they stretched His arms along it.

Rabbi shifted, wincing with His mouth open as His back slid against the cracks of the tree, but He still made no sound. The soldiers felt around His wrists for the delicate space between the bones. Pressing their thumbs down into His wrist to mark the spot, they reached into their tool kits and brought out two nine-inch wrought iron nails. They held them up like daggers and shoved the tip atop each wrist. One of them took a hammer clung to his belt. With unsteady stabs of cruelty, he nailed Him to the rugged tree—and then he handed it to the other soldier. He took his turn, forcing the nail into Rabbi's wrist. The sound of crushing bone meant he missed, but he didn't care. He hammered over and over until only the head of the nail remained.

Rabbi clenched His teeth, convulsing, and His eyes rolled to the back of His head.

I couldn't breathe. The faint sound of His moaning showed He was trying to hide His pain. My only guess was that even at His most vulnerable, He wanted to protect me, His mother, and anyone else who loved Him from hearing His complaints of excruciating pain. I had never seen anything like it.

Within seconds, a third soldier knelt at the foot of the cross and stretched out Rabbi's feet. He arranged one on top of the other and swung the hammer through the air, forcing His feet into one. Then he fixed a sign, sent from Pilate, to the top of the cross. It read:

JESUS OF NAZARETH, THE KING OF THE JEWS.

The onlookers came and read the sign, which was written in Aramaic, Latin, and Greek. One who saw it gasped and ran off—no doubt to warn the leaders—but Pilate had instructed them to fix it to the cross. I hoped he had enough of their persuasion for a lifetime.

Their brutal work was over, and several soldiers gathered together. Using Rabbi's body as leverage to lift the cross, they dropped it into a hole. Rabbi's tacked body flung forward, hands held above His head, His weight in His shackled feet, and His caved stomach stretched out, void of air.

Mary ran to His feet. Embracing them with her cheek, she wept. She brushed them across her face.

A centurion threw her back toward the crowd. "Get out of here, you!"

We looked up at Rabbi. Pressing down on His broken feet and the nail supporting Him, He slid His wounded back across the jagged surface of the tree, inching upward to draw in a single half breath. Collapsing back down, He exhaled.

There was nothing I could do. He was surrounded by the enemy. They stood there, staring—waiting for Him to get too tired to lift Himself—and waiting for Him to suffocate. I held Mary and Mother, one on each side of me. My tunic was wet with their angst.

"My Son. My Son," Mary said, hyperventilating.

I refused to cry. He was up there, fighting for every breath and struggling up and down.

People passing along the road jeered and shook their heads in mock lament. "You bragged that You could tear down the Temple and then rebuild it in three days—so show us Your stuff! Save Yourself! If You're really God's Son, come down from that cross!"

Rabbi prayed, "Father, forgive them; they don't know what they're doing."

The Roman soldiers took His clothes and divided them up four ways, to each soldier a fourth, but His robe was seamless, a single piece of weaving, so they said to each other, "Let's not tear it up. Let's throw dice to see who gets it." Dividing up His clothes, they threw dice for them.

Moments later, Zedekiah and Shet came. Standing there and smirking, they were right there mixing it up with the rest of them, having a great time poking fun at Him: "He saved others—but He can't save himself! King of Israel, is He? Then let Him get down from that cross. We'll all become believers then! He was so sure of God—well, let Him rescue His 'Son' now—if He wants Him! He did claim to be God's Son, didn't He?"

Behind me, someone screamed, "No!"

Someone else shouted, "Help me!"

The soldiers brought two more men to be crucified. Neither had experienced the flogging and brutality of Rabbi. Once crucified, their crosses were put into holes, and though bound to their deaths, they joined in the taunting Rabbi.

One cursed and said, "Some Messiah You are! Save yourself! Save us!"

The other one made him shut up and said, "Have you no fear of God? You're getting the same as Him. We deserve this, but not Him. He did nothing to deserve this. Jesus, remember me when You enter Your kingdom."

Rabbi lifted His head from His chest and whispered, "Don't worry. I will. Today, you will join Me in paradise."

Though it was only midday, the sky dimmed until it turned black. It was the kind of moment when I was sure my dream of the rider named Death was real. He was here, coming for his prize: Rabbi. I looked up at the cloudless sky, expecting him to ride across it, but there was only darkness and nothing to explain why. It didn't take long for most of the crowd to lose interest and head back to town. Those who loved Him stayed on the hill.

Rabbi continued rising and falling for each breath.

The Marys and I knelt in prayer. If anyone could save Him now, it was God Himself. Time stopped, or at least it felt like it did, and we prayed.

Rabbi broke the silence and cried out, "*Eloi, Eloi, lema sabachthani? My God, My God, why have You abandoned Me?*"

My question was the same. *Why did He not come? Why did God leave Him to a gruesome end?* It was the first time I had heard Rabbi be uncertain. I didn't know what it meant.

A remaining bystander sneered and said, "Listen, He's calling for Elijah."

He didn't know Rabbi. He didn't understand.

No one came. Nothing happened.

Rabbi looked down at me. At first, I wasn't sure, but then He said to His mother, "Woman, here is your son." He said to me, "Here is your mother." I knew what He was asking of me. With His head bowed, Rabbi rasped, "I'm thirsty."

A jug of sour wine was standing by. Someone put a sponge soaked with the wine on a javelin and lifted it to His mouth.

Rabbi sucked the bitter liquid. "Father, I place My life in Your hands!" Then He breathed His last.

The earth shook. Stones rumbled beneath my sandals. It quaked until we could no longer hold ourselves upright. We fell on one another. Screams and bouts of terror covered the hilltop. There was no rain, no sign to describe the sudden shaking. Rocks split into pieces. At the foothill, I could see a hand atop an open grave, but the chaos distracted me. Before I could see the grave again, something or someone crawled out from it.

The captain of the guard proclaimed, "This has to be the Son of God!"

The rumbling settled, and we clamored to our feet. My eyes were glued to Him. No rising or falling of His chest. No movement. Nothing, only death. He hung there, a shattered version of His once joyful self. Destroyed by hands of hate and jealously—tied by false doctrine and lies—yet He was free.

I stood. Resting my hand on Mary's shoulder, I braced my shaky knees—afraid to join Him. The very thought of a world without Him was too painful. I hated them. All of them. None of them would love Him no matter how hard He tried. Nothing He said changed their hearts, and now He was gone, but in death, He conquered them. In death, He was safe.

One of the centurions saw Rabbi's lifeless body and said, "This Man was innocent! A good Man, and innocent!"

He was too late. No one could help now.

CHAPTER TWENTY

alone

I knelt in the dirt of the place that stole my rabbi—my face hidden in my hands. Something that had once been far away, loomed over those watching: Death. He had come like a soft voice, barely heard, in the blink of an eye, but Rabbi went willingly, leaving an emptiness in the pit of my gut. It seemed impossible for the black to win a victory over the Son of God, but Rabbi hung on a cross above me. Death had torn the veil of good, uncovering the leaders' jealousy and misguided self-promotion.

It was over. Finished. At least in Death's grasp, no one else could hurt Him. He was God, shrunken down for us into human form, but the world did not receive Him—could not.

Standing, the Marys and I went to Him. Mary Magdalene touched His foot with the tip of her fingers. "They hated themselves— not You, Rabbi," she whispered.

We stood there for a moment in the patch of dirt beneath Him. Their weeping filled my ears, but I couldn't. I had to take care of them—take care of His mother. Rabbi asked me to be her son. I was responsible for her now. She was as much my responsibility as my own mother.

I heard the clopping noise of more soldiers' boots coming up the hill. My heart began to race. Without a word, they went to the criminal crucified at Rabbi's side, still clinging to his life. "No … don't … please!" the man wailed at them. We knew what they intended.

It was policy, the religious sort. No one could hang on a cross during Passover. It made us look bad as a people, barbaric even, but we were far worse.

Swinging a club through the air, a soldier crushed his legs. The criminal's scream followed the sound of his breaking shin bones. It was no use. Without his legs, he couldn't lift himself to breathe. He panted, trying to use every last bit of air, and we watched the life leave him.

They did the same to the second criminal, but he was promised access to Rabbi's kingdom. He winced in pain, but he forced a smile as he let go—ready to see Rabbi on the other side.

Poking my head between the fourteen soldiers huddled together, I waited to see what they would do to Rabbi. One of the soldiers drew his spear. Lifting it, with a single motion, he stabbed Rabbi between the ribs. Blood and water gushed out.

Just as I was about to lunge at the solider, someone called, "John, son of Zebedee?"

I froze—afraid to be me. I didn't know who I could trust. I turned around, hands up.

"I'm Joseph, from Arimathea. You are John?"

I stared at him.

"I am a member of the council. Do you remember me?"

He looked the same as they did: old and sour.

"You're one of them?" I asked.

"No, no I'm different, John." He pressed his hand to his gray cloak. "I never consented to their decision, this heinous cruelty." He gazed up at Rabbi. Looking away, he added, "You see, I was called by Nicodemus, another secret follower—from inside the Sanhedrin. We knew this was coming. We tried to turn others among the seventy-one." He sighed. "They would not see reason. Caiaphas can be very convincing, and they were afraid of losing their standing. It was—"

I tuned out his words. I wanted to kill him—them. The hate boiled up inside of me, and I saw myself pushing him off his knobby knees down the hill, but the Romans wouldn't stand for my insurrection. I fixed my eyes at Rabbi's feet, laying there my anger, frustrations—everything left in me.

"John? You see, we have gone to the prefect."

"Prefect?" I asked.

He looked at Mary and then quickly back at me. "Yes, he—Nicodemus—together we asked for permission to bury your rabbi. John, you're the man here now. We need to know if we might bring Him to a final resting place."

"You went to the prefect?" It didn't make sense for them to care.

He leaned in. "Secretly, yes—we went to the praetorium to ask the prefect if we could bury Him."

I scoffed. "*Secretly?*"

"Nicodemus and I, with shielded faces."

"Why hide? You're one of them," I said.

"They are looking for you—for the twelve and anyone who knew His words."

"Me?"

"To destroy what is left of His teachings."

My heart sank. "Are the others alive?"

"I do not know, John."

I shifted my mind. "Nicodemus? I remember him. He came one night, asking Rabbi about rebirth."

"Yes, yes! The very one. Nicodemus shared with me what your rabbi said. It was unlike anything I had ever heard. And I remember the words well. 'Unless a person submits to this original creation—the 'wind-hovering-over-the-water' creation, the invisible moving the visible, a baptism into a new life—it's not possible to enter God's kingdom. When you look at a baby, it's just that: a body you can look at and touch, but the person who takes shape within is formed by something you can't see and touch—the Spirit—and becomes a living spirit.

"So don't be so surprised when I tell you that you have to be 'born from above'—out of this world, so to speak. You know well enough how the wind blows this way and that. You hear it rustling through the trees, but you have no idea where it comes from or where it's headed next. That's the way it is with everyone 'born from above' by the wind of God, the Spirit of God'."

"Rabbi tried to warn him about the leaders, but it didn't do any good."

Behind me, someone said, "It did. It will!"

"Nicodemus, you have returned!" Joseph said, going to him.

I clenched my teeth.

There he stood with the same dark hair and eyes Rabbi had. They could have been brothers—should have been—but his robes showed he wasn't from the humble world Rabbi had belonged to. "Shalom, John."

I nodded.

Nicodemus looked around the silent hill and then up to Rabbi. He sighed. "I know this is hard for you, John. That night, He told me the truth of it. I did not understand then what I do now." He came closer and crouched a bit. Looking me in the eyes, he whispered, "I remember it like it was yesterday. He said, 'This is how much God loved the world: He gave his Son, His one and only Son. And this is why: so that no one need be destroyed; by believing in Him, anyone can have a whole and lasting life. God didn't go to all the trouble of sending His Son merely to point an accusing finger, telling the world how bad it was. He came to help, to put the world right again. Anyone who trusts in Him is acquitted; anyone who refuses to trust Him has long since been under the death sentence without knowing it. And why? Because of that person's failure to believe in the one-of-a-kind Son of God when introduced to Him.' This is not over."

I didn't know what to say. I stood there, trying to take in Rabbi's words, knowing He was gone.

Joseph said, "Do you have the prefect's decree?"

"I do." Nicodemus turned away from me, went to the lead soldier, handed him something sealed, and then returned to us. "It is time."

"Why? Why help Him now? Why speak His words now, but not when He needed you?" I asked.

"I lacked the courage." He looked down at his sandals. "I learned vastly more about my role as a leader shadowing Jesus than I had in all my years alone. And like many, I was drawn to the characteristics I shared with Him—a desire to change the hearts of the leaders. I saw their corruption, but I never said anything—or did anything. I might be an old man, but, John, I was afraid. A coward. I wanted to hide, like so many, like the rest of the twelve, but I know the truth of who He is. He has given me the power to speak out, which I hope to do now. We need to get Him down, John, and give a proper burial."

Joseph came behind him. "It is the least we can do for not intervening in His conviction."

"We want only to bury Him, John. To give Him a proper place to rest," Nicodemus added. He looked at Mary.

I looked at her too. It was time. I nodded.

He signaled the soldiers. They gathered around Rabbi, lifted the cross from the hole, and rested it on the ground. Crouching over Him, they removed the nails and then parted way, allowing His mother to go to Him.

Mary ran to Him, collapsed at His side, and wept. She shook as she reached out for His hand. Taking it, she swept it back and forth across her cheek. "My heart. Rest, my Lord."

Mother was silent. Walking to Mary, she looked back at me and gave a faint lift of the corner of her mouth. "You can do this, John," she whispered as she helped Mary rise.

Nicodemus, Joseph, and I went to Him. Kneeling, I closed my eyes for a moment. I knew it was time, but I couldn't. I was hoping it wasn't real—that He wasn't gone. It was too awful to be the truth. I hadn't untangled myself enough to tell Him the worst part of me: my dreams. I thought I had more time, but in a moment, He vanished. I was a liar, a fraud—hiding behind our friendship—but I never really told Him who I was. I never got to say that I was alone, a half-empty person riddled with loads of shame and regret.

He loved me, catered to me even—taught His simple truth over and over—but it never penetrated my thick skull. I didn't see, but my eyes had been opened. I wished that everyone else would vanish in His place—that I could have one more moment to tell Him how much He meant me.

I opened my eyes to the isolation. The red sun set, separating me from the rest of the world. The remaining passersby, looking rather upset, made their way down the hill.

"John, are you ready?" Joseph asked.

Touching His head, I felt deep despair, hollowness. I sighed, knowing we had to be careful with the loose skin surrounding His torso and legs.

In his satchel, Nicodemus uncovered a bottle and strips of linen.

Pouring it out, the scent of myrrh and aloe disguised the odor of blood. He soaked the linen strips and handed them to Joseph and me. We took turns turning Him side to side, and He slipped through my hands. He was cold and constricted, but my loyalty enslaved me to diligently try to tend to Him. My heart was beating, interrupting the order of my task. I was so consumed with my dreadful guilt that I didn't realize I had tightened my arms and legs so much that when we finished and needed to stand, I fell back onto my knees.

"John, you can do this," Nicodemus said. "We are finished."

"Let us carry Him to my tomb nearby." Joseph wiped his brow, transferring a mixture of blood and oils to his head.

"Your face," Nicodemus said, handing him a piece of cloth. "John, you carry His legs, and we will carry His shoulders."

I slid, scrambling clumsily to His feet, and Nicodemus and Joseph went to His shoulders. We heaved, swinging His body toward us, and He felt lighter than He should—or maybe the thought of dropping Him turned up my strength. Steady as we could, we held Him, dignified, followed by the Marys.

The journey felt nothing like the joyous ones I had with Him before all this. Instead, the somber walk of death reminded me of my demented dreams. Halfway down the hill, I saw the garden and the new tomb. Even the mountain that held the tomb dreaded His arrival. We entered the cutout, walking past the great stone rolled beside the entrance. I looked down at Him, knowing I was moments away from never seeing Him again. Everything we shared seemed to belong only to the past.

In the center of the tomb, a slab was waiting for Him. We laid Him down, and Mary seized her moment. Going to Him, she quivered over him, muttering like they were the only ones in the tomb. She whimpered, "Farewell."

When the others finished their goodbyes, I went to His side and leaned over His shoulder. His pale face showed through the crumpled linen. "Rabbi, I don't want to leave You."

It was still the day of preparation with the Sabbath about to begin, and there was no time to waste—no other option. Before I realized it, I was walking away and had crossed the threshold of the tomb. Taking one last look, I wanted to go to him—to say something—but there were no more words. I knew in my grief that He could rest, undisturbed.

The three of us pushed the giant rock, sealing the entrance carved into the center of the mountain.

Mary's voice trembled as she said, "Son, come home with me. I will give you something to eat. And we will prepare spices and perfume more oils after the Sabbath."

At least I had somewhere to go for the night. I wasn't sure how safe it was to be with her, but I didn't care anymore. My life felt so pointless. I conceded and followed them.

"Thank you, John," Nicodemus said.

Joseph said, "We will find you when the time is right. Stay hidden. Stay safe."

"It is not over yet. We will need to prepare Him properly later. Good night. God is able, and there is still hope, John, son of Zebedee," Nicodemus said.

They turned and left.

As we walked to the home of Mary, the word *hope* echoed in my mind.

After a small supper, I went to the loft and took off my tunic and belt. Throwing them on the floor, I kicked off my sandals, fell onto a mat, and lay down. It wasn't long before my gift opened me to another world.

In my dream, I saw an angel. He was dressed in clean, bright linen and wore a gold vest. He called out to me and said, "Come here. I'll show you the Bride, the Wife of the Lamb." He took me away in the Spirit to an enormous, high mountain and showed me

Holy Jerusalem descending out of heaven from God, resplendent in the bright glory of God.

The city shimmered like a precious gem, filled with pulsing light. She had a wall, majestic and high, with twelve gates. At each gate stood an angel, and on the gates were inscribed the names of the twelve tribes of the sons of Israel: three gates on the east, three gates on the north, three gates on the south, three gates on the west. The wall was set on twelve foundations, the names of the twelve … inscribed on them.

I sat up and shouted, "James … Peter!" My brother and my friends were missing, hidden somewhere.

Then something came over me. I realized my dream was of heaven, angels—the ultimate creations, vibrant and alive. It wasn't over. Things were only beginning. His words flooded my mind with great urgency. "Everything written in the Prophets about the Son of Man will take place. He will be handed over to the Romans, jeered at, made sport of, and spit on. Then, after giving Him the third degree, they will kill Him. In three days, He will rise, alive."

In all my misery I had misunderstood—and I had completely forgotten that everything He said would happen did. I sat in the darkness of death, hopeful. He would rise.

It was as clear as the rising sun shining through the window and crawling across my mat that a new day had come. He will rise meant death wasn't the end. I tossed off my blanket, shot to my feet, and screamed, "He will rise again on the third day!" I shoved my head through my tunic with one hand and swung my belt around my waist with the other. I shoveled my sandals with my feet and gripping only the ladder's rails, I slid down, skipping the rungs. Landing on both feet on the bottom floor of Mary's house, I shouted, "He will rise!"

The Marys were huddled near the stove and preparing a Sabbath meal. His mother said, "What did you say, John? Who will rise?"

"He will rise!" I shouted. "On the third day. That's what He said—what He promised!"

"Who?" Mary Magdalene said.

"Rabbi. My rabbi. Your rabbi!"

"You must be so tired, my son. Please rest."

"No! Mother, you don't understand. I didn't understand at first, but I do now. He will rise."

"You have said that, but what does it mean, John?" the mother of Clopas asked me.

Hesitating for a moment, I answered, "I don't know exactly, but He will. He said so." They weren't giving me the reaction I expected, and I didn't know the details, but I just knew He was going to rise somehow. Even though I couldn't explain it, I felt it. I believed it.

They stared at me, and Mary said, "Your mother is right, John. You need to rest. It has been … difficult."

"I can't. I have to find my brother, to find Peter. I have to give them hope. I have to remind them of what Rabbi said. He *will* rise!"

I grabbed my satchel and hurried to the table where they had laid out fresh pomegranates and dates. I snatched a few and tossed them inside. "I have to go. I will come back for you all. Stay hidden. Stay safe." I went to Mother and kissed her cheek.

Bursting through the door, I shut it behind me and squinted at the sun. I sighed and took off running, glancing over my shoulder. I didn't care that it was the Sabbath. I didn't care who saw me. I needed to get to them—wherever they had gone—and remind them of what He had promised. Out of the city gates and into the wilderness, I ran to find the rest of the twelve.

ABOUT THE AUTHOR

U.E. Wall lives in Texas with her husband and five girls.

ABOUT THE ILLUSTRATOR

Justine Peterson is a watercolorist with a distinct blend of pencil and charcoal, allowing her to push the gesture of her illustrations and fine art. Her portrait and figurative works capture active emotion and awaken the spirit—resonating with its viewers. Justine lives with her husband and three boys in Southern Utah.

REFERENCES

The Baptizer: John 20:31; Matthew. 3:1–3; John 1:7, 17–18; Matthew 3:7– 8; John 1:20, 22–23, 25–27, 30–31; Matthew 3:14–15, 17; John 1:38.

The Messiah: Psalms 115:3; Matthew 3:11.

The Call: Matthew 4:19; John 1:42.

Following Him: John 1:43, 45–51; Revelation 13:7–12; Luke 4:43.

Demons: Deuteronomy 6:4–5, 13–14; Matthew 5:13–20; Matthew 6:5–8; Mark 1:24–25, 27.

Miracles: Matthew 6:25–27, 31–34; Mark 1:38.

Healing: Luke 5:12–13; Matthew 9:2–3; Mark 2:4–7; Leviticus 24:14–16.

Sermon on the Mount: Matthew 7:1–2; Mark 7:3–5; Luke 12:4–7; Mark 2:16–17; Matthew 12:2; Exodus 35:2–3; Matthew 12:6, 17; Mark 2:27.

The Twelve: Revelation 1:12–14; Mark 3:26; Matthew 12:28–30; Mark 3:28–30, 33–35; Matthew 10:5–8, 9–10, 11–27, 32–33, 40.

Five Thousand: Mark 6:31, 34; Matthew 14:4–5; Mark 6:19–25, 27–28; Matthew 11:11–19, 21–30; Matthew 14:15–16, 18; Mark 6:37–38; John 6:5–7, 9–10, 12.

The Sea: Mark 6:50, Matthew 14:28–31, 33; John 6:25–38, 42–58, 60–65, 67–70.

The Transfiguration: Matthew 12:38; Matthew 16:2–4, 13–19; Luke 9:22; Matthew 16–22; Luke 9:23–27; Mark 9:4–5, 7, 9–12, 16–17, 19–25, 28–29, 31.

Pharisees: Matthew 10:34; Matthew 20:21–24, 26–28; John 7:13; Matthew 12:1–12; John 7:15–20; John 7:25–29, 31–32, 34, 36, 40–43; John 8:21–26, 31–59.

Satan: Matthew 4:1–11; John 10:24–30, 32–38; Matthew 20:30–34; Luke 8:1–3.

Lazarus: John 11:3–4, 9–12, 14–16, 21–23, 25–27, 32–34, 39–44; Mark 14:6; Matthew 21:2–3, 6–11; John 12:22–36.

Betrayed: Matthew 21:13–14; 16; Mark 14:13–14; John 13:6–12, 18–21, 26–27, 31–38; John 14:1–31; Matthew 26:36; Mark 14:34–36; Matthew 26:40; Mark 14:42

A Dark Night: John 18:5, 7, 9; Matthew 26:49–50; Luke 22:48–49, 51–54; John 18:20, 22, 24; Mark 14:56–57, 60, 62, 65, 67–70; Matthew 27:3.

Pilate: John 18:29; Luke 23:2–4; John 18:30–32; Luke 23:5, 10, 13-16; Mark 15:4–5; John 19:7, 12, 14-15.

The Cross: John 19:16–19; Luke 23:29–30; John 19:19; Matthew 27:40; Luke 23:24; John 19:23; Luke 23:25; Matthew 27:41–43; Luke 23:39–43; Mark 15:34-35; John 19:25; John 19:28; Luke 23:46; Matthew 27:54; Luke 23:27.

Alone: John 19:34; John 3:5–8; John 3:16–18; Revelation 21:9—14; Luke 18:32–34.

Printed in the United States
by Baker & Taylor Publisher Services